Pagan Metaphysics 101
The Beginning Of Enlightenment

Rev. Vickie Carey, D.D., Ph.D./Springwolf

Schiffer
Publishing Ltd

4880 Lower Valley Road   Atglen, Pennsylvania   19310

Text and images by author
Cover photo: Menhirs At Night © Anyka. www.bigstockphoto.com
Title Page photo: © Audrr. www.bigstock.com

Library of Congress Control Number: 2011933101
Type set in Garamond Cond.

ISBN: 978-0-7643-3897-7
Printed in United States

Schiffer Books are available at special discounts for bulk purchases for sales promotions or premiums. Special editions, including personalized covers, corporate imprints, and excerpts can be created in large quantities for special needs. For more information contact the publisher:

Published by Schiffer Publishing Ltd.
4880 Lower Valley Road
Atglen, PA 19310
Phone: (610) 593-1777; Fax: (610) 593-2002
E-mail: Info@schifferbooks.com

For the largest selection of fine reference books on this and related subjects, please visit our website at
www.schifferbooks.com
We are always looking for people to write books on new and related subjects. If you have an idea for a book, please contact us at
proposals@schifferbooks.com

This book may be purchased from the publisher.
Include $5.00 for shipping.
Please try your bookstore first.
You may write for a free catalog.

In Europe, Schiffer books are distributed by
Bushwood Books
6 Marksbury Ave.
Kew Gardens
Surrey TW9 4JF England
Phone: 44 (0) 20 8392 8585; Fax: 44 (0) 20 8392 9876
E-mail: info@bushwoodbooks.co.uk
Website: www.bushwoodbooks.co.uk

Dedication

This Book Is Dedicated
With the deepest love and appreciation
To My Boys
Garrett and Aidan

Acknowledgments

I would like to thank four important ladies who gave their knowledge and helped me along my path:

Shirley MacLaine, "Out On A Limb"
Rev. Beth Gray, Reiki Grand Master
Rev. Michele Lusson, D.D., Author and Teacher
Rev. Wilma Donald, Reiki Master

Contents

Introduction

The study of spirituality has long been an interest of mine. I was drawn to paganism at a fairly early age and began serious study when I reached adulthood. This interest has taken me on a long and fascinating journey into many different paths of spirituality.

Throughout my travels, I've had an opportunity to explore Christianity and the Methodist approach to religion. I've explored Native American Shamanism, Celtic Shamanism, Metaphysics, New Age Metaphysics, and of course Pagan Metaphysics and Magick. I've been blessed with the chance to learn from some wonderful teachers and fellow students along the way—implementing those practices that ring true within my own conscious thought, as well as, experimenting with those that don't. Sometimes changing their approach slightly to fit in my world, while discarding the rest. In the end, what doesn't fit can be set aside and left for others to find. But all have an influence and impact to my personal approach to my own spiritual world.

I've discovered that some of the concepts I've come across, really are part of me and dwell deep within my being. Not all of the concepts can be proven by science nor can you provide proof of their ultimate existence. But through your own research, study, and personal experiences over the years, you find validation, confirmation, and develop the proof you need in understanding your own spirituality. For me, that's what faith is all about. It is the journey, not the destination.

Along this journey, I've been given the opportunity to teach and lecture a variety of people from new to experienced practitioners. Sharing what I've learned and practiced, and still discovering new things and possibilities from those I encounter, has been just as interesting as when I first started my journey. I've also been honored and somewhat surprised by the number of people who have been interested in what I have to say. After many years of constant encouragement from my best friend and partner, I finally sat down and comprised my years of research and study into writing.

Let me be the first to say that there are many ways to approaching Pagan Metaphysics. These concepts are not new or original. They are merely a culmination of my personal research, education, and experiences. But if you're interested in the beginning and basic concepts of Pagan Metaphysics, how it can be used in your life, and how it can bring about positive change, then this book may lead you to your own interesting journey and help you on your way to your own spiritual enlightenment.

Along with the information and insights contained within these pages, I hope to provide thoughtful exercises that will help the reader experience the concepts described herein. I strongly suggest you begin your own Educational Grimoire [a textbook of magick] to keep notes, document your thoughts and record your own experiences—if for no other reason than it allows you to keep a personal testimony of your journey for future review and reference. But writing things down also helps you fill in the blanks, identify your own contradictions of belief, and work out for yourself what you really subscribe to on your spiritual path and how it all fits together.

This information and the exercises are designed to empower YOU. It is to help you learn how to go within, connect with your own Divine Spirit, communicate with the greater Divine Consciousness, and bring a sense of spiritual wholeness to your being. Through this process, individuals can walk through every moment of the day with a sense of higher purposes, greater connection to their spiritual mission, and with insight to meet their personal and spiritual goals.

I hope you find it helpful. I hope it can fill some gaps or open new avenues of thought and perceptions that you may not have thought of before. And even if you don't agree with the information contained within this series, maybe it will provide new or alternative concepts to things you have not yet thought about on your own spiritual journey. Or perhaps this spiritual perspective will provide insight to the avenues of belief held by others around you. And through this perspective, the teachings may bring about tolerance and peace between religions and spiritual beliefs.

Many Blessings,
SpringWolf

Where To Begin

What Do You Believe?

Before you can begin a spiritual journey, what ever that journey is, you have to know where you're starting. What do you believe and how does it relate to your spiritual path in the here and now? Are you looking for a spiritual path or a religion? Are you looking for a structured path, or an open-ended belief system? Are you just

looking for a place to fit in, but don't know which one fits your current beliefs? How are you going to assess where you are today with where you want to be if you don't know what you believe in at this moment in time?

It's easy to sit down and answer questions off the top of your head when talking with someone about what you believe. Or to sit in your comfortable reading chair and say to yourself, "I know what I believe." But in approaching your beliefs in this way you will jump from topic to topic or skip over concepts that connect your beliefs together. You may not even realize how subjects are interconnected during your conversation. You can give one description today about a concept and two weeks from now, you'll have a slightly different description for the same topic and you may not even realize that you provided a different definition or altered your view or perception.

You may say, "I believe in reincarnation." Okay, but how does it work? Seriously think about how the spirit is different from the soul. Do you know? How is the soul connected to the physical body? What happens when the physical body dies? When you say you believe in reincarnation, do you have a full understanding of what that means and how it works? As you study the concept, the details you discover may change your opinion.

The first assignment to any spiritual journey is to write down what you believe right now. You'll discover how much that *easy to answer* conversation suddenly becomes a little more thought provoking and may not be as easy as you thought. But don't let the potential of difficulty stop you from writing. When you're putting thought to paper, you are forcing yourself to really think about what you believe, how your concepts are interrelated and support each other. You will also take your spiritual journey to a new level of deep understanding, tapping into the energy of your own soul and spiritual mind to define what you believe.

You'll discover which concepts seem to have gaps and which ones seem to contradict other things you thought you believed or knew. You'll begin writing an answer to a question you were sure you knew the answer to, only to discover that you may not be so sure about it after all. Writing forces you to connect the dots. You'll find that as you're writing an answer to one question, you might contradict your response to another question. And suddenly, you have to re-think an entire subject and it's overall concepts.

It's important to keep in mind that there are no right or wrong answers. Nor is there a deadline or time frame for when these questions have to be answered. The point to these questions is to make a person think about the details of their beliefs and to provide a starting point for the spiritual journey ahead. As you learn and research, you will come back to these pages and update, change, or even totally re-write your first set of answers. So keep your original answers. Copy them when you update or rewrite.

If there are topics you don't know anything about, leave them blank. Those unanswered questions provide you with a list of "to be researched" topics. Jot them down and carry them with you. You'll find yourself making little notes on those topics that can help lead you to resources that further your research.

Regardless of your level of knowledge and development, however, this assignment can be beneficial. Keeping a record of your beliefs helps you see where you started and later on provides a record for how much you've grown and expanded your awareness. You will also discover that you really do know much more than you think.

Put Your Beliefs In Writing

You're going to start a journal separate from everything else you have in your library. You can consider this part of your *Spiritual Journal* or *Grimoire*. The best thing to do is get a spiral notebook or, if you're like me and you type faster than you write, you might start a document on your computer. You can always print off those pages and put them in a binder later. If you don't print them, make sure you have a back up of the document on a CD or flash drive! There's no way to emphasize the importance of backing up your digital research and journals.

Whatever you chose, you're journal is going to be organized as follows:

(I suggest you read this entire assignment before you begin writing.)

1. On the first page, write the date and your name.
(Whatever that "name" is to you). You get no other explanation than that.

2. On the next page, give your notebook a Title.
"What I know I know," "My Spiritual Evolution," "My Spiritual Grimoire" — whatever suits your fancy.

3. The third page begins your first section of beliefs.
These are the topics you're sure you know and you're confident in your understanding of these concepts. Start the section by writing a list of topics and their definitions. Where you start is up to you. But you will want to keep the definitions to about 4 sentences each. You're not writing a reference manual here, just basic ideas/concepts.

4. In the second section, cover "What I think I know."
Do the same thing as before, write the topics and a short definition. This section is what you think these things are and what they mean to you at this point in time. But they are things you're not totally sure about, or perhaps you think something is missing from your perspective.

5. The third section is "What I'd like to know."
Here you'll just list topics. Think of this as a reading list for future research.

6. And finally, the last section is for "Walking My Talk."
What do you think your spiritual path is and what will you do to implement that in your daily life. Walking your talk is part of walking a spiritual path. They are not separate from each other.

By writing all this down, you'll see that what you think you know, can sometimes contradict what you know you know. So you'll have to rethink some of your perspectives or change your topic from one section to another for further research. In writing what you don't think you know anything about, you will discover you do have some ideas, just by sitting for a moment and thinking a topic through.

Sample Questions

Now, if you prefer to simply answer a list of questions, here's a few things you'll want to answer in your topic/definitions. I've tried to make these as generic as possible, but keep in mind that many of these questions assume you believe in reincarnation and basic metaphysical theories such as karma, energy, and alike. If you don't, then simply skip those questions in your journal, or go ahead and say you don't believe in that particular topic and why.

1. What is the Divine?

2. What is God/Goddess and is this different from the Divine?

3. Where do we come from? Think creation versus evolution. What do you think?

4. What is the spirit?

5. What is the soul?

6. Is the spirit and soul the same thing?

7. Do you believe in reincarnation? If so, define what it is to you. Is it reincarnation, transmigration or Rebirth?

8. What is transmigration and Rebirth?

9. How does each new incarnation come to be? (I'm talking spirit here, not the physical process of procreation.)

10. Do you have past-life memories? If so, where are these memories kept?

11. How do these past-life memories affect this lifetime?

12. How can you use these past-life memories in this lifetime?

13. What is the purpose of an incarnated life? What are you here to do?

14. Is the soul related/connected to the physical body? If so how? Define both spiritual and physical connections.

15. Where does the soul go once the physical body dies?

16. Do you believe in karma? If so, define it.

17. What is Kundalini?

18. What are chakras? And how are they related to Kundalini?

19. How are the chakras related to the soul?

20. Do you believe in spirits? If so, what are they?

21. Do you believe in ghosts? If so, what are they?

22. How do ghosts differ from spirits? Or do they?

23. What are spirit guides?

24. What are animal guides or animal spirit guides? Is there a difference?

25. Are there other different kinds of guides? If so, list and define them.

26. What is energy?

27. What is setting protection? And why is it important?

28. What is an aura?

29. What are spiritual senses? Do you have one?

30. What do you think about psychic abilities? Do they exist or are they helpful?

31. What do you think about spiritual healing? Does it exist?

32. What do you think about meditation? What are the benefits of meditation, both physical and on a spiritual level?

Lastly, the ultimate question to any spiritual path is:

Why are you walking "this" path?

1. What do you want to achieve from your studies? (I'm not talking about talents; I'm talking about spiritual knowledge and enlightenment.)

2. What do you want to achieve or do with your knowledge? This is more of the physical activities. And it could include talents (such as psychic abilities, healing, or teaching).

3. How are you going to apply this knowledge to your daily life?

Once you have your answers written down, you're ready to begin your personal journey. As you learn and discover new concepts and ideas, you may want to come back to your questions and review your answers. Discover if any should be updated, or totally changed. Fill in the blanks between concepts that you had with what you have learned along the way.

You may notice there are no questions about typical pagan concepts, such as magick, spell craft, calling quarters, and alike. Those topics are for a later book in this series. Here we are just concerning ourselves with the starting point and foundation of metaphysical concepts.

This section of your journal should always be a work in progress, as we never stop learning and never stop growing toward our own enlightenment.

Metaphysical Basics

What is Metaphysics?

Metaphysics is the philosophical study of first-cause principals. That's a fancy way of saying: "How the Universe got started." There are two areas of study to consider when looking at metaphysics. The first is Physics itself.

Physics is the study of the observed world. What we can see, touch, manipulate, and observe the results of those manipulations. The manipulations can occur either by natural forces or by physical interaction or interference.

The word "meta" means higher and beyond. Here we're talking about the concepts beyond physics. Thus metaphysics is the study of the world beyond physical observation. In this definition, Metaphysics is a philosophy of physics that tries to solve the questions that material science cannot.

Metaphysics is the study of life beyond physics, between physical and spiritual observations. Where did we come from? Who are we? Why are we here?

New Age Metaphysics

New Age Metaphysics is a period of time in history, where human consciousness has been drawn back into it's own spiritual awareness. This cycle period has been prophesized by many famous psychics such as Nostradamus, Edgar Cayce, Lazarus, and others as the time of great spiritual evolution. It has been described as a time when the human consciousness is given the opportunity to rise up to the God Consciousness, or fall behind and be consumed. Many Christians would call this time period the preparation for the second coming of Christ. New Age believers might refer to it as the awakening of the Jesus Consciousness or Christ Consciousness. Still others may refer to it as the Aquarian Age.

The marble bust of Aristotle is a Roman copy of the bronze original
by Lysippus. It is housed in the Ludovisi Collection
Creative Commons – Attribution-ShareAlike

New Age Metaphysics combines the concepts and theory of first principals (the science) and the New Age cycle ideals (the faith). It is a balance between what one can test and prove through physics and what one can experience and prove through metaphysics. In other words, it is a combination of known physics and scientific understanding combined with what an individual believes internally as their personal truth.

This time period is also called the next evolution of the human spirit, where the world moves from "Survival of the fittest" to "Survival of the most spiritual." But don't take that to mean there's only one path or religion that has the dominant voice of being the "most spiritual." There are many paths to choose from.

Survival of the most spiritual is not a sect or group. It's a personal path that is created by an individual's own personal choices and moral creed. Are you living "true" to your own spiritual path? Are you *Walking Your Talk*?

Pagan Metaphysics

Pagan is defined as any religion that does not espouse to the doctrine of Abrahamic religions. That means any religion that bases its belief system on Abrahamic doctrine, such as Judaism, Christianity, and Muslim faiths along with all their variations and off shoots.

Pagan beliefs existed long before the labels of "metaphysics" or "pagan" or "neo-pagan" were created. If you can get past the creation of the labels, and focus on the ideals; Pagan Metaphysics is a balance of physics through the observation of the natural world. It is a path that follows the laws of nature but takes those practices a step further and builds the spiritual foundation of belief on metaphysical principles.

There is little difference between Metaphysics and Pagan Metaphysics. The main diversion between the two paths come from the view of positive (good) and negative (bad) events and their energy or associations. While Metaphysicians, and especially New Age Metaphysicians focus on the positive, they very often don't even acknowledge the negative. Or if they do, it's to acknowledge its existence in order to avoid it or work to keep it away from one's spiritual path or journey. Many call this a focus on white light and purity.

Where as, Pagan Metaphysicians not only acknowledge the negative, it sees this side of nature as being required to create balance in all things. Without it, there is an unknowing of what "positive" is or means. This doesn't mean pagans focus on negative actions. It merely means, pagans acknowledge its existence and recognize its value in certain situations.

This concept carries through in many of the perspectives of Pagan Metaphysics from energy to honoring the Divine Consciousness through celebrating the duality of nature through the ideals of the good and bad, positive and negative, or white and black aspects—in rituals and practices.

If you think of this in terms of chaos and creation, it makes a little more sense. A forest fire can be seen as a bad situation, destroying wide ranges of land, plants, property, and lives—both animal and human. But out of the ashes of a forest fire comes a new vital element that returns nutrients to the ground and brings forth an explosion of re-growth. Out of chaos comes the creation of a new forest.

Pagan Metaphysics acknowledges the chaos and destruction and recognizes the creation that springs out of the ashes. Seeing both as equal energies through out the universe and creation. Both are vital in nature just as they are in human life. Sometimes we must close one door in our lives in order to open another which leads us to greater understanding, peace, or takes us to the next level of our spiritual mission.

Is Metaphysics A Religion?

Because many religions today profess to be metaphysical in nature, many people understand the word Metaphysics to be a general philosophy and not a religious sect. Metaphysics underlies many philosophies, some sciences, and much literature. In most dictionaries and encyclopedias, metaphysics is listed as a philosophical doctrine that defines "all things are part of each other and searches to discover first cause principals." But because it defines a doctrine of spiritual creation, evolution, and existence, it can be both a philosophy and a religion.

When applied to a spiritual practice, Metaphysical philosophy can become a religion unto itself. It defines it's own set of beliefs, it's principles characterize a Divine order, and it identifies practices designed for individuals to become one with the Divine Universe around us. It is these things (order, principals, rituals, and worship) that define a religion.

But that doesn't mean the philosophies can't be utilized by others to build upon for their own concepts and implemented through their own specific rituals and ceremonies. This is the case of New Age Metaphysics and Pagan Metaphysics. Both are very similar in understanding, but both choose to take their own paths and detail some concepts that the other does not.

When Did Metaphysics Begin?

Let's start with the word *Metaphysics*. In the scheme of life here on Earth, the word is fairly new. Coined in the late 300s B.C. by Aristotle, this advanced thinker and philosopher had written and titled a book about *Physics*. This work dealt with the knowledge of physical science for his time. It is the study and theories of physical law that revolves around the "observed world." Almost immediately after the completion of *Physics*, Aristotle began his next work, *Metaphysics*. This one was a continuation of the first, but where physics looked at the observed world, metaphysics looked at the underlying meaning and structure of the unseen world.

From Aristotle's point of view, Metaphysics asks: What are space and time? What is a thing and how does it differ from an idea? Are humans free to decide their fate? Is there a first cause, or God, that has made everything and put it into motion? All the basic questions that humanity has struggled with since the dawn of time.

After his death, many of Aristotle's writings vanished or were scattered throughout Western Europe. By the Middle Ages, the only articles known to exist were his writings of Logic. These writings became the basis of the 3 Medieval trivium: logic, grammar, and rhetoric.

By the thirteenth century, more writings were found and were eventually translated into Latin. The best-known writings are:

- "Organon" (treatises on logic)
- "Rhetoric"; "Poetics"
- "History of Animals"
- "Metaphysics"
- "De Anima" (on psychology)
- "Nicomachean Ethics"
- "Politics"
- "Constitution of Athens"

Who Started This Philosophy?

While Aristotle wrote what many consider to be the first works of Metaphysics, it wasn't an original philosophy that he established or created. He had his predecessors to thank for that. We can look to the Egyptians, Aztecs, and the cultures of the Orient and Native American Peoples as well and see much of the same philosophical approaches—some of which certainly existed long before Aristotle's time. But his knowledge came from many other Greek thinkers such as Pythagoras, Socrates, and Plato who were his teachers. We can briefly follow their teachings and discover Aristotle's history into Metaphysics.

Certainly Pythagoras had some influence in the concepts set down by Aristotle. He established the Pythagorean Brotherhood, around 530 B.C., which was dedicated to reforming political, moral, and social life within the society based on their spiritual views. Sadly, the Brotherhood came into conflict with the seated government, and rather than face trial for heresy, Pythagoras disbanded the brotherhood and fled his homeland. Much of his work on these spiritual subjects was destroyed and he became known primarily as the Great Mathematician who created the Pythagorean Theory. But oral tradition and writings from many of his students carried his concepts forward under new labels and titles.

One example was Heraclitus who is sometimes called the Weeping Philosopher, or the Dark Philosopher. Heraclitus studied the theories of Pythagoras and expounded upon them with his own perceptions. Because of this, he is often called the founder or Grand Father of Metaphysics.

Some people say Plato is the founder because of his work in philosophies and sociology, which was, based on the work of his predecessors Pythagoras and Heraclitus. Aristotle was a student of Plato, and wrote the book on the subject, so he is also credited with being the originator of Metaphysics.

But if you look at the world as a whole, the same struggle to understand and search for the "meaning of life" was everywhere around the globe. The Egyptians had a pretty well-defined set of philosophical and spiritual beliefs long before Aristotle. Plato gave rise to his views of an ancient culture that was divinely cultivated when he wrote of the legendary Atlantis and its spiritually structured society. The pre-Incas and Aztecs were both cultures that were embodied with spiritualism and mysticism of equal proportions to those written by the Greek scholars.

We can't discount the in-depth insights and teachings from Asia either. There is a great deal of metaphysical philosophy from Confucius and Buddha. We also see these concepts in early Hindu belief structures as well. And no we can't discount the teachings from the Hebrews nor early Christians for their contributions.

We can examine all ancient cultures and find components of metaphysical philosophy embedded within their societies. The concepts were there long before anyone started putting them into writing or using them as a teaching tool. But most historians give the main credit to Aristotle. In my view, however, it's important to remember that he didn't come up with the concepts on his own. He gained this knowledge through his own education and learning from others. They gleaned their understanding from those before them and they from earlier teachers before them.

Metaphysics 101

In the Beginning

From a Pagan Metaphysical perspective:

There are many names for the Divine Consciousness. The Great Spirit, God, Goddess, the Divine Spirit, "The All," "The Everything," the essence of everything in the universe. For the purpose of this writing we'll refer to this essence as the Divine Spirit.

Most every religion has some type of story about the beginnings of life. Metaphysics is no different. There's no way we can ever know how long this took, if it was an instant, or a million years. But the creation of the physical is held in the divine memory that we all have within us.

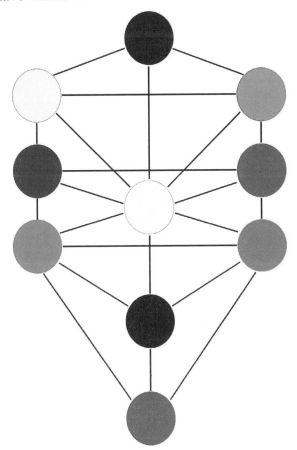

In the beginning, there was conscious energy. This energy evolved and became self-aware, evolving into the Divine energy. Through its progression of existence, the Divine energy became an enlightened Spirit and discovered the ability to create. From its own essence, the Divine Spirit created a physical presence out of the nothingness. There was no light, no distance, space or time. There was just thought that formed the very first Divine creation.

The Divine Spirit was pleased with what it had done and the expansion of the physical presence began. The presence flowed and moved, turning and creating the building blocks of all matter. This matter teaming with energy began collapsing in upon its self until one day out of the physical creation of the Divine Spirit a monumental explosion occurred. This material matter flew out moving at great speeds and with amazing energy. Creating the first light of the Divine Universe. Life began to form as elements of this matter exploded like a phantasm of light and movement. Stars were born and out of their birth, Galaxies were formed and the vast expansion of space came into being. Planets evolved and moved through the newly created galaxies. Some settling perfectly near a giant star, others fading and crashing only to find death in the chaos of Divine Creation.

Those perfect planets slowly progressed through the chaos and in their own time and through their own influences of water, air, and light, life grew. Through this evolution, the spark of the Divine Spirit was held within all these creations, because they came from the Divine energy itself. They are part of the Divine, because they are from the Divine.

Through the story of Metaphysical creation, we have the concepts of spiritual belief (The Creation) meeting modern human science (The Big Bang and subsequent evolution). Metaphysics teaches that each of these, science and belief, are the same thing and we can see that here. In Metaphysics we believe that evolution started from Divine touch and intervention. And through the Divine Chaos of the Big Bang, evolution ensued and is held within each of us today.

Dr. Stephen Hawking has said, "If you have a gold ring, appreciate it. Because held within its metal structure is the energy of creation." These are the same components that are held within you and me. Where all of creation got its start, is within each of us.

The reason "God" is in all things is because the Divine Spirit used a part of itself to create all things. I alone am not the Goddess and you alone are not the God. But you and I and all things in and around the Divine universe, seen and unseen, known and unknown, all that is, makes up what the Divine is. We are not separate or apart from the Divine Spirit. We are all part of the Divine Spirit, part of each other, connected, intertwined, and alike. All that is, is the Divine Consciousness of the Universe held within the collective Divine Creation. And that is held within our own super consciousness that connects us to each other through our connection with the Divine Consciousness. We are one through spirit.

Soul Groups

Also Known As Star Groups

The universe evolved and progressed in varying stages and at various speeds. As this evolutionary process moved forward, many Soul Groups formed in star systems far away from ours. Through their evolution, these civilizations grew into advanced societies, learning the balance of spirit and physical incarnation.

Their evolution in other star systems established the alternate label "Star Groups." Some prophets suggest the Divine Spirit influenced these evolutionary advancements. Others believe their enlightenment was merely the normal cycle or process of life. Change happens and change is inevitable. Through evolutionary change, enlightenment can be achieved.

Many believe that each of these groups or advanced civilizations brought a specific understanding of spirituality and life into the universe at the height of their evolution. Even though science doesn't support these hypotheses, information gathered from many channeled readings by prophets like Edgar Cayce, Seth, Lazarus, and others, have consistently provided information about these

Soul Groups. In addition to the Past-Life research that has been documented extensively by mainstream scientists such Dr. Raymond Moody, Dr. Frank Alper, and others, we can gain a picture of these early civilizations and how they influenced life here on Earth.

Along with these prophets and scientists, a myriad of metaphysical practitioners have developed the hypothesis that suggest the impact of the Soul Groups upon the evolution of Earth began over 600,000 years ago. Many also agree these Soul Groups were collectively referred to as the "Army of Spiritual Development." Who gave them this name is unclear.

What *is* clear is the evolution of life here on Earth was beginning to form into a spiritual intelligence. Whither by chance or Divine intervention, each of these Soul Groups came to Earth with a specific purpose or mission of knowledge to aid in this evolutionary process. But the reason for their coming is somewhat elusive.

Here are a few of the many hypotheses concerning this concept. You can pick the one you like the best, or do some of your own research and add to the list:

1. Some prophets say the coming of the Soul Groups was needed to speed up the evolution of the human consciousness. But they fail to explain why this speedy evolution was or is needed.

2. Some prophets suggest the Soul Groups wanted to share their enlightenment with the human species in order to share the knowledge and avoid the same pitfalls they progressed through.

3. Some theories suggest we are fallen Gods, who have been banished from the Divine conscious mind for the misuse of divine power and Godly sins. Our progression along our spiritual path is a means of redemption and a progression to return to the God consciousness. The Soul Groups were sent by the Divine Spirit consciousness to aid in this redemption process.

4. Some suggest the Soul Groups were so advanced that they simply formed a scientific expedition to examine the evolution of life into an intelligent being on a primitive planet. And that planet just happened to be Earth.

5. And finally some suggest this coming was pre-ordained. The Divine Spirit's way of integrating all the created civilizations into one melting pot, so to speak. To bring all the talents, knowledge, wisdom, and universal energies together into one collective conscious mind. Again, a type of experiment to influence the evolutionary process here on Earth.

This last idea would support "Earth, the Great experiment" hypothesis, which permeates the teachings from many spiritual religions. Each of these hypotheses suggests we are the descendents of or the culmination of the work influenced by these early Soul Groups. Some suggest that many of us alive here today could be the reincarnation of beings that came to this planet on this mission designated by the Soul Groups, handed out long ago. Until that mission has been accomplished, we will continue reincarnating here on Earth.

So who were these Soul Groups and where were they from? We have come to know these groups as the 5 Enlightened Civilizations. Each one named for its place of origin within the Divine Universe, bringing a specific order of knowledge and talent to the grand experiment.

1. The Ontarians

These are the Humanitarians. They come to teach love and compassion. They are credited with being the rescuers of the Atlantis survivors here on Earth.

2. The Cyrians

These are the teachers of Order. They bring to us the knowledge of science and law. They teach us to put order into things, in both physical and spiritual terms.

3. The Polarians

These are the teachers of Balance. They teach that everything in life exists in balance in both the physical and spiritual realms.

4. The Antarians

These are the Pathfinders. They bring us the lessons of both astronomy and astrology. Helping us to find our way through the cycle of life.

5. The Pleiadians

These are the Bridge Builders or the spiritual teachers. They help us learn how to build the bridge between the mental and spiritual minds.

This mission of spiritual integration began after the evolution of humanoid beings here on Earth. As the Soul Groups incarnated into human form, they slowly worked their influence over the natural evolution that was already taking place. This method provided them with a mechanism to bring their knowledge and purpose to Earth where they could be shared with all the created species in a common manner.

Each progression of human evolution is built on the previous cycle or the previous civilization's knowledge. Each of these evolutionary civilizations became known as the Root Races or the Roots of Human Evolution.

Root Races

Simply put, Root Races are significant and specific points in history where humankind reached a pinnacle of development and knowledge. We can identify 7 generations or 7 Root Races of human evolution.

The First Root Race

The essence of life on Earth begins. From the ameba to the first land mammals, this is the point where life began.

The Second Root Race

This was the time of Lamouria. This was the first race that was half human and half animal, where we slowly learned to think and respond to the observed world.

The Third Root Race

This was the progression of evolution in Lamouria. During this time, life slowly discarded the animal natures and moved from reacting on instinct to reacting through thought and intelligent decisions.

The Fourth Root Race

The "perfection" of Atlantean wisdom and knowledge comes into play. Some prophets suggest the establishment of the Atlantean culture here on Earth greatly influenced the evolution already taking place. And this time period was a grand leap from Lamouria to an evolved human culture.

Others suggest the Atlantean culture was not part of the Root Races here on Earth at all, and instead, they were people from a neighboring planet that was being destroyed. They escaped this destruction by immigrating to Earth. Instead, they point to the Essenes as the fourth root race. The Essenes were a Jewish religious group that flourished from the second century B.C.E. to the first century C.E. They are believed to be the people who wrote the *Dead Sea Scrolls*.

The Fifth Root Race

As a result of the destruction of the perfection of Atlantis, Earth's evolution loses wisdom and knowledge. As war broke out between the people of science and the people of spirituality on Atlantis, many of its citizens fled to varying parts of the world— taking their knowledge and wisdom with them, and influencing the knowledge of the civilizations they migrated to. During this war, the knowledge of creation and evolution was destroyed.

The Sixth Root Race

This time is known as the New Age of humanity. Some prophets say this began during the time of Jesus. Others believe it began as spiritual religions found a footing in their own cultures and regions of the world were established, developing their own concepts and beliefs independent of each other.

The Seventh Root Race

This is where we are today, in the here and now. In 2008, the cosmic cycle renewed and the world entered into the first phase of the seventh evolution of humankind. What many have labeled the "Universal Human."

How Atlantis Influenced the Root Races

The integration of the Soul Groups into human evolution really took footing from the time of Lamouria 400,000 to 100,000 years ago. Channeled information, research from Dr. Frank Alper and Dr. Raymond Moody provide a large pool of information about this time period.

The next major leap in human evolution occurred about 80-60,000 years ago, when a nearby planet was threatened with extinction. Many of its citizens were chosen to evacuate in order to establish a survival of this species on another planet. These evacuees came to Earth, dismantling their ships in order to build their society here on this planet.

The Atlanteans believed, "God is one, not separate and distinct," according to Dr. Frank Alper, a renowned researcher of the Atlantean society. This belief lasted until about 25,000 B.C. when Atlantean science began to progress faster than their spiritual accountability. They began to abuse their spiritual power and their egos grew a bit to big for their britches. As the movie line goes: "They were so busy trying to find out if they *could*, they didn't stop to think if they *should*."

It appears the main angst was in the misuse of scientific knowledge in the realm of DNA and DNA splicing—something the Atlanteans were apparently very good at. Their perfect society was being corrupted by this practice, as new species of humans were being created and segregated from the "higher" or "pure" humans. Many believe ancient mythologies of monsters or half animal/half human creatures are based on these scientific experiments. The Centaurs (half human, half horse beings) are an example of this DNA splicing. Along with winged humans, and other failed combinations of human and animal species that can be found in mythologies around the world and seemingly unconnected to other mythologies of the same slant.

The segregation between these "mutant" beings and evolved humans was of great concern to the Spiritual side of the Atlantean society. Which was also the governing body of Atlantis. Through political power, they began to set rules and laws upon the scientists and their actions. Of course, this was not well received by the scientists. Thus a power struggle quickly ensued resulting in a war between the spiritualists and the scientists. The war they created quickly destroyed their society and their land. Some suggest the scientists created a massive weapon made of giant crystals that some how backfired and destroyed the continent, causing it to break apart and sink into the ocean.

As a result, the Earth was cast into a vacuum, a punishment of Divine intervention. Quarantined if you will, keeping out any new waves of information or visitations from other planets where life had formed and evolved. In the physical sense, this quarantine came in the form of the Van Allen radiation belt. The Atlantean destruction crystallized the human evolutionary process, almost stopping our growth. The only communication between Earth and the other universal energies was in the form of messengers, what we've come to call Angels.

The de-crystallization of the human spirit slowly began about 6,000 years ago. But until this century, the quarantine was still very much in place. Around the 1800s, we as a society, reached a point in our karmic debt gained in Atlantis and the veil of forgetfulness has slowly been falling ever since. There was an increase in space visitation and an increase in Angel communications. This increase in communication brought with it a huge explosion of spiritual enlightenment, which can be seen in waves of progress during the late 1800s when many metaphysical groups were being formed in mainstream society. And again during the 1960s to 1980s when a second wave of spiritual thinking hit western cultures. These waves of progress continue today in metaphysical and pagan communities, while mainstream religions struggle with inner turmoil and conflict between each other around the world.

The other side effect to the Atlantean crystallization was that it trapped some of those teachers from the Soul Groups here on Earth. Those "teachers" got caught up in that ego and greed and in the scheme of things; they gained some of their own hefty karma for their interference. So if you feel as if you were part of one of these Soul Groups, perhaps you are. Souls trapped here began their restitution for their interference and began guiding the human spirit back to its evolutionary status. We are told that these souls played a big part in the establishment of "The Initiation Schools," which were the civilizations that focused on spiritual "remembering."

The Initiation Schools

The Initiation Schools were civilizations where people lived in the purest form of their spiritual beliefs in a specific point in time in history. These civilizations participated in evolution and karmic repayment gained during the destruction of Atlantis and the negative interference of the Soul Groups. These efforts were significant to advance the individual human spirit, as well as, human society as a whole.

Many of the spiritual teachers of today were people who lived during these special times and participated in the creation or existence of these civilizations. These souls took on a mission to work through karma and re-learning their spiritual mission in order to help prepare our society for the "New Age" evolution.

There were seven original Initiation cultures. But there were also several sub-cultures in between these time periods. An individual soul that lived through all these initiation schools would be considered a Master Teacher today. That includes people like Jesus, Krishna, Buddha, and others in history. Today it would include people like Pope John Paul, wise preachers or Rabbi's, enlightened individuals, such as Edgar Cayce, Doreen Valiente, Starhawk, Shakti Gawain, Billy Graham, Joel Olsteen, and many others. Even though these teachers cross religious boundaries, they each bring a message of hope, inclusion, and living the values of their own teachings. Something we know not all spiritual teachers aspire to, or actually do. They bring the knowledge of faith through love and tolerance, not obedience by fear. And that's a significant difference.

It's important to note that even though many religions hold different views on the specifics of creation, human evolution, and living a spiritual life, we all have a basic foundation of belief that is the same. We are all trying to live the best we can, in the most loving and spiritual way we can, in order to attain evolution of the spirit. Whither that evolution is believed to be to the next level of enlightenment, or getting into Heaven doesn't matter. We are much more alike than we are different. And we are all trying to advance the human soul toward enlightenment, just as the Initiation Schools have tried to do.

Who and Where Were These Civilizations?

1. Tibet
They opened the original vortex to prepare the energy and set the base for work to begin. They brought in the healing techniques and the science of life.

2. Early Egyptian Dynasty

They brought in the expression of art and culture. They helped to establish the "order" and structure of living in a community.

3. Sumerian

They helped to define the communication between societies with the structure of language and the written word.

4. Pre-Mayan

They contributed architecture, community building, and the science of designing. Further setting a base for the evolution by defining a structure for planning.

5. Pre-Incas

They brought in the traditions of community, a sense of legacy and culture. Along with understanding the knowledge of responsibility to each other and to society as a whole.

6. Anazazi

They contributed environmental awareness; the knowing that "God" connects all things together through spiritual consciousness.

7. Essences

A Jewish community who contributed the form of teaching to society. Some researchers also believe this community was responsible for the creation of the Master Teacher Jesus.

There are also sub-initiation schools. You might think of them as summer schools, or schools of continuing education. The Greeks, the Incas, and the early civilizations of the American Indians fall into this category. All these communities were equally spiritual in their daily living and held similar beliefs concerning humankind and our place in the universe. These civilizations were the societies that put into practice what the Initiation schools taught. Even though many of these schools may have been barbaric in our terms today—don't forget that even in the Bible, we can find great acts of barbarism—they held a deep spiritual thought and practice to their everyday living. The acts of violence shouldn't diminish the contributions of these societies on the spiritual "re-evolution" of the human spirit.

How Do These Schools Affect Us Now?

The role of a spirit who participated in these civilizations is simply "a person who is willing to take the steps toward Atonement." Or a better way to say it: To Reach for At-one-ment with the Divine Spirit.

This means taking on the lessons and choices that will lead a spirit to enlightenment and to become one with the Divine Consciousness again. It's a huge commitment to take on the responsibility and lessons of enlightenment. And doing so generally means taking on the role of spiritual teacher. Providing knowledge, wisdom, and guidance for others who are also seeking enlightenment, is part of that process.

Through Atonement, Resurrection, Transformation, and Service to community or humanity, these Initiates have helped and continue to help the progression of the human spirit along its enlightened path. They are the teachers, healers, Shamans, Ministers, Priests, and Priestesses who teach empowerment, who freely share their knowledge and their experience with others. The key to this role is Empowerment.

People who claim the title "spiritual teacher, advisor, or clergy" must provide information and guidance without control. Everyone must face their life and spiritual choices on their own terms and make their own decisions for moving forward. So a spiritual teacher, who makes demands upon their student in the form of control, is taking away the ability of their student to reach for their own spiritual evolution.

It is through free will and choice that we walk the path toward enlightenment and attain At-one-ment. No one can learn these lessons or live these concepts for us. We each, no matter what religion one walks, must take control, responsibility, and accountability for our own spiritual life. We can become empowered to find the Divine Spirit within ourselves. Or we can allow a fake teacher to control our choices and give up our free will to advance.

The Initiation Schools helped human kind continually advance through the cosmic cycles of progression. Each spiritual society provided energy or contributions of knowledge to the karmic lessons being learned and atoned for. This contribution of energy continues today. These cosmic cycles of progression are specific periods in time where specific energy is focused for specific lessons and issues to be addressed on both a personal and global spiritual perspective.

Cosmic Cycles

Every religion and belief system has its own mythos about the cycle of life, which includes Divine Creation or the beginning of life, the evolution of life, the end of life, and the return to Spirit. In the simplest of terms, this is the Cycle of Life.

In metaphysical terms, the Divine Universe and everything in it also moves through a cycle of change. This Cosmic Cycle not only affects us as individual beings, but as a collective consciousness as well. The Cosmic Cycles started when time started. This was the beginning of all life throughout the Divine Universe.

Cosmic Cycle Periods

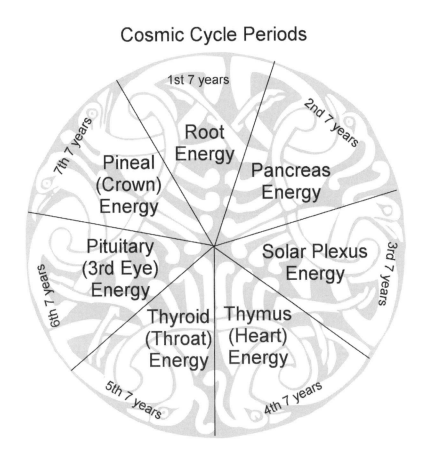

Just like incarnated beings, the Divine Universe also experiences patterns of energy, which fluctuate between major and minor changes. These moving patterns of cyclical energy generally last a certain period of time (about fifty years here on Earth). The entire period of change is called the Cosmic Cycle. There are many other names for this process; Divine Cycles, Spiritual Cycles, Soul Cycles or Chakra Cycles are just a few.

These cycles are stages of time affecting the energies of a specific chakra within the "soul body" of the cosmos, which in turn influences Galaxies, planets, entire civilizations, societies within those civilizations, and even individual living beings.

The Chakras are energy vortices on a sub-atomic level. Also called Energy Centers, these vortices respond to specific types of movement and influence. For instance, the Thyroid chakra center affects the throat area of an individual being. This is also called the "will" center or the center of choice.

When we as individual beings are working on lessons of choice, putting into action what we say or think on the physical level, we stimulate this energy center located in our throat. In turn this center influences the choices we face on a spiritual level. How will we work through an experience that impacts a spiritual lesson designed to repay or redeem karma, or to break a pattern carried over from a previous lifetime. The choices we make affect more than just the physical experience we see. It also affects our soul and spiritual progression toward enlightenment.

The Universe and all its physical components are also affected in a similar way on a greater spiritual stage. How a country or even a corporation responds to a traumatic event is also an exercise of will and choice. And just like individual beings, these larger components of the Cosmos also face lessons on a spiritual and karmic level.

We cannot work on all the issues or energy patterns all at once. And there is a structure and organization to the Divine Universe. Thus as a collective Divine consciousness, we have periods of time to focus on specific areas or lessons. Narrowing down the responsibilities and accountabilities to a more manageable level, so to speak. This occurs with the progression of energy through the Cosmic Periods.

The Cosmic Periods

A complete Cosmic Cycle contains 7 areas or periods of cosmic growth and influence. These are often referred to as the Cosmic Periods. Each period moves through a progression or evolution of energy and influence for 7 years.

As we progress through each cycle period another one begins. When we finish one set of cycle periods, we "graduate" so to speak to a new level of energy and the cycles begin again. Energy is always moving, continuously flowing, evolving and influencing the seen and unseen Divine Universe around us, as well as, within us.

Each period brings with it a different level of work to be done based on the chakra center being influenced. We face these energies as we do all things in our lives, with free will and choice. These are not preordained, but they are pre-structured opportunities. We can only try to achieve the goals set within the structures by making the right choices. Otherwise, we risk the chance of sliding backwards and repeating the lessons provided in these time periods at another time. Either later in this embodied lifetime, or in the next reincarnated state.

The Seven Areas of Cosmic Growth

1. Root Energy

Each new Cosmic Cycle begins with the Root Center. This is the security center of consciousness. It embodies the basic needs for physical health, well-being and survival.

2. Pancreas

The next Cosmic Period relates to the Pancreas Center. It governs how we honor and maintain our physical nature in balance with our spiritual responsibilities.

3. Solar Plexus

The next progression relates to the Solar Plexus. This time period fosters the co-creation between the soul and the Divine Universe. It governs how we manifest experiences in the physical world that can provide us with opportunities of spiritual growth. Of course as individuals, governments, companies, and societies, we can make bad choices and limit the growth or even take a step back and "de-evolve" so to speak.

4. Thymus

We migrate to the next Cosmic Period of the Thymus or Heart. This energy pattern governs the union between the spiritual and physical natures in harmony, love, and compassion. On a personal level, we may face times of unconditional love, self-love, or compassion for others. On a global level we may face issues of tolerance, peace, or resolving conflict.

5. Thyroid

The next cycle period deals with the Thyroid. This is the Will center or the center of choice. This is where the communication of physical choices (what you say or want to say) comes together with the physical choices you make (what you put into action).

6. Pituitary

Moving to the next period we face the issues of the Pituitary. This is the period of spiritual revelation, where the gateway to the higher self becomes available and open. It reflects the oneness of the individual spirit with the oneness of the collective Universal Divine Spirit. On a global level this could be seen as facing lessons for how we treat our fellow humankind.

7. Pineal

The last period in the Cosmic Cycle is Pineal energy. This energy pattern governs the ultimate state of awareness. It influences how we feel about our connection to the cosmic consciousness, the Divine Universe and all things in and round it. Do we see ourselves as us against them? Or as connected living beings, a part of each other and linked through Divine energy?

The Current Cosmic Cycle

The last Cosmic Cycle began in 1958 and ended in 2007. In 2008 we started the next 50 year Major Cosmic Cycle and the first of the 7 year Minor Cosmic Periods. Try to compare these descriptions to events that occurred during the same time frames and see if you can make a correlation between the cosmic energies and the events.

2008-2015 Root Energy

Once again we enter a Cosmic Cycle in war. As with the last cycle we moved from the "romantic" era that surrounded those wonderful old war movies, and stepped into the true horrors of what war really is during Korea and the Vietnam War. That cycle repeats itself in this period, but on a different scale. As we move into the cycle of the Universal Human, we step from "survival of fittest" to "survival of the most spiritual." Consequently, our global society has stepped into a period associated with a Holy War of religious righteousness. In this stage of our evolution, we are working on learning that spirituality is not grounded in one path, but rather it's ground within ourselves. The root period is telling us to set a foundation on which to build upon. It is our home center from which we will progress through the remaining periods of this complete cycle. But the "home" building here, is building our own inner spiritual center or spiritual home within our own individual selves.

Sadly, we haven't done very well on a global level to accomplish this lesson and alter the pattern of intolerance. Just a few years into this cycle, and it appears we have fallen back on old fears and prejudices to enact selfish righteousness.

2015-2022 Pancreas Energy

In this period, we face the lessons of learning how to accept each other for who we are. Paying more attention to our similarities rather than our differences. Through the hardships of the past period, we learn that accepting each other and honoring the spirit of all in respect and celebration is key to creating the sweetness of life. At this time, there will be those who refuse to let go of the past and continue their protests. But their voices will not be as loud, and in many cases, they will be but whispers as the global environment pulls together to bring back peace and happiness.

2022-2029 Solar Plexus

Transformation and Creation are the energies that are at work in this cycle. The effects of "green living" will be the paramount position of industrialized civilizations. Even if the governments don't follow suit, the overwhelming benefits in both life and business will take hold and move forward. The planet will always be here, but it's up to humankind to decide if we will be here or if we will continue to destroy the resources we have been afforded. This time period will bring with it amazing advancements and creative solutions to age-old issues and problems.

2029-2036 Thymus Energy

While human kind has learned the "politically correct" view of honoring all, many voices have not put their actions where their mouths have been. During this time, the synthesis of spiritual and physical natures will either collide or they will generate efforts to truly put into practice the unconditional love of all.

Sadly it's likely that some regions of the world will choose to collide into violence giving rise to a potential new war. They will appear to be angry that their views are minimized and not taken seriously. Like little children throwing a temper tantrum. Their actions, however, will not last for long. The rest of the world has evolved into tolerance and will not stand for persecution based on ideological ideas and prejudices. The rebellions will be easily put down, though the voices of angst may not be silenced.

2036-2043 Thyroid

We attempt to rise above the needs and desire of control, which have merged, into spiritual control over humankind. Choices will be presented that provide for an increase in peace, or a sliding back into aggressions based on religious beliefs.

Communication, and not strength of will, is the key to success in this period. Learning to listen, instead of assuming "I know best" and "just do what I say and all will be okay." Here the desire to control on both an individual level and a global governmental level must be restrained. Acceptance of other cultures and perspectives must be exercised in order to achieve the greatest avenues of communication.

2043-2050 Pituitary

For those who continued to walk their spiritual path in honor, peace, and respect, this time brings a great celebration of spirit. Similar to the Aquarian Age, those who survived the test of the "most spiritual," will find rewards as yet unrealized. This will affect both the physical and spiritual world. Individuals will attain a new perspective of vision and will look beyond the limitations they are accustomed to. Governments will achieve the ability to see beyond their borders and open their eyes to the vast Universe around, below them in the seas and above them in the stars.

2050-2057 Pineal

The Beginning. The cycle renews and prepares us for the next Cosmic Cycle. Those who have not moved onto the spiritual path will be left by the wayside. They will face hardships and struggles unseen in previous ages. They will be forced to atone or be left behind in confusion and limbo. Those who have prepared for this time will move on and enjoy the fruits of their labor, sharing in the expansion of the spirit with newly discovered and unexpected partners.

This Cosmic Cycle wraps around the next major evolution of humankind, known as the Universal Human.

The Universal Human

In 1958, we entered the evolutionary cycle of the Human soul that opened a huge doorway to spiritual thinking. From 1958 to 2007, we progressed through the cycle of what many call the Aquarian Age. It is a time in our history where we can see an evolutionary explosion of spiritual thought and understanding around the world. But especially here in Western cultures we gave witness to a huge array of needed and required changes to bring humankind back

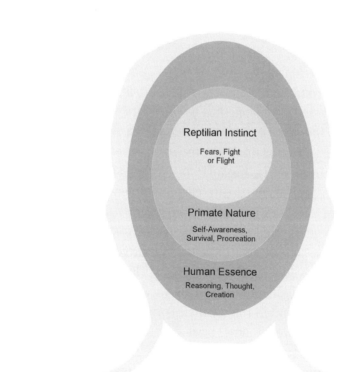

Reptilian Instinct

Fears, Fight
or Flight

Primate Nature

Self-Awareness,
Survival, Procreation

Human Essence

Reasoning, Thought,
Creation

into balance with the Divine Spirit. Think of the expanded interest in Angels, Channeled knowledge, meditation, holistic healing, and spiritual accountability, and you can see the renewed awareness within the human spirit. But you can also see the advancements made to bring balance between races, the sexes, and even cultures and societies.

While there have been pockets of resistance, with very loud voices overwhelming the majority of conscious thinkers, the past cosmic Cycle has been a period of reawakening. In the face of that loud opposition, we have seen an increase of ideas, a rebirth of old information, and a sense of inner knowing about the Divine Spiritual knowledge we all have within ourselves. These activities have set us up for the next cycle of spiritual evolution known as the Universal Human.

The Universal Human is a period in time based on the metaphysical concepts built from the Beginning of Creation, inspired by the Soul Group integration and implemented by the Root Races. Some see this time period as the point where "Humankind can get back on track" with the original plan or original experiment of evolution.

Unfortunately, we're not off to a great start within this evolutionary cycle. The increase in religious intolerance and extreme fundamentalist activities is perhaps a knee jerk reaction of fear to the changes in energy felt on a Cosmic level. From a metaphysical perspective, these acts are creating a great negative karmic impact to this cycle. As many hold up their banners or rifles and proclaim their religious path as the one and only true way to Divine acceptance, they will be left behind in the spiritual Divine dimension. It doesn't matter which path you follow, be it Pagan, Christian, Muslim, or some other form of spiritual belief. What will matter is how you live within balance and honor to all others around you within this world existence. We must learn to be human and humble in our humanity, so to speak.

Our Evolution – Who Are We Humans?

We are the culmination of both creation and evolution. Metaphysically speaking, we are not just the creation of a divine being, nor are we totally the result of scientific evolution. But rather we are combination of both. The Divine Spirit created the Universe from its own being. In doing so, it put a piece of itself in all things — including humans. The Divine then influenced the evolution on Earth through the Soul Groups and Root Races.

The result of this was Divine evolution that established the nature of human kind. We can see this action in our own human natures. At our core, humans have three internal natures that have merged together during this evolutionary process.

1. Reptilian - The Inner Most Layer

The first molecule to form and rise out of the sludge of the earth by the touch of Divine energy was reptilian. From this center of our being, we carry this stage of evolution with us. Our instincts, fears, and courage come from this nature of ourselves.

2. Primate Nature - The Center Layer

As our evolution progressed, so did our natures. We began moving onto land and experiencing life and more of the nature of ourselves. At this point, our Primate essence came into being. We discovered self-awareness and the ability to create in our own right. From this nature we learned about emotions, power, family, and the desire to procreate.

3. Man - The Outer Most Layer

Our evolution continued and we moved from mammal of the animal, to the mammal of human kind. During this time period, we began learning how to Think and Respond to the world around us. It is at this level where the human essence learned to use creative energies for more than just family or survival. Here we step onto the creation level of the Divine and began to influence the world around us with our limitless imagination. In other words, we began creating the world around us, instead of just living in it.

Continued Evolution

We are still evolving to the next level of being as the Universal Human. It is important to note this is an evolution of being into spirit. Moving in progression from physical beings creating the world around us, to spiritual beings who are not limited by physical constraints within the world around us.

All over the world, people are beginning to open up their awareness and thought of spiritual balance and knowledge, utilizing knowledge gained through the Initiation Schools and throughout history to progress their way of thinking, living and being. This new perspective sets old fears to rest, empowers us to share knowledge and ideals, provides opportunities to advance not only our social existence, but also to advance our limitless possibilities beyond the physical world.

This evolutionary cycle comes to teach us about our abilities we have not yet tapped into. Those who have not already learned about the ability to connect to the Divine consciousness on a daily basis will discover knowledge and information to help them advance not only on a spiritual level, but on a physical, social, and perhaps even an economic level as well. From here we can span our physical consciousness, through our soul consciousness, to our spiritual consciousness, which is the bridge to the Divine Consciousness and make new discoveries we couldn't have dreamed of before.

On an individual basis, we learn to look at the world and the events around us from the larger Divine perspective. We can understand why things happen or present themselves to learn spiritual lessons or work on karmic issues that will help us to evolve our soul and attain enlightenment. This isn't something that will happen over night, or even in a few years. But rather it is an evolutionary process that will allow us to see and understand the energy of the mind, and abilities it has that we have not tapped into as yet.

Here we are talking about the utilization of Divine energy and our ability to connect to Divine creation. Currently, science says we only use a small portion of our brains to think, reason, and act. The evolution of the Universal Human will increase that ability exponentially as we tap into the deeper resources of our whole consciousness. From here we will take the next steps to advance our spiritual being and as a result improve our physical condition.

The Spiritual Realms

As with anything, there are many ideas about the levels of the ethereal or the spiritual realms of the Universe. The most common concept comes from non-pagan beliefs of Heaven, Earth, and Hell. Wither or not they exist in the ethereal realm can be up for great debate depending on who you talk to. A Christian will say *yes they exist.*

Metaphysics takes a different view. To most Metaphysical and Pagan followers, Heaven and Hell are what you make of your life here in this incarnated lifetime. You can create your own hell right here on Earth. Consequently, you can create your own heaven as well.

This view is based on the concept that there is energy on all levels of existence. These levels are interconnected and can be traversed through birth and death transitions, or through communications between souls and spirits.

Some suggest the levels of the ethereal realm coincide with the existence of the multiple universes that science believes it has proven to exist. What is often called the multi-verse. These parallel universes exist on different energy levels and can be seen when each side alters its energy to open a gateway so to speak and connect to another level. Think of it this way, in order for us to communicate with spirit we must heighten our energy vibration. But at the same time, the spirits we want to communicate with must slow their vibration down a bit. When these two vibration patterns are in synch, a pathway is opened and communication can take place.

Metaphysical concepts, written long ago, define a hypothesis that there is a structure and order to these multiple-dimensional realms of existence. These realms make up the Divine Universe.

The Divine Universe

The Divine Universe is divided up into levels or realms of existence. Some call these the seven Kingdoms of Enlightenment. A soul progresses through these levels based on their choices and actions in both spirit and physical form. How quickly they progress depends on the karma they have earned and repaid, the spiritual lessons they have learned and the knowledge they have gained toward enlightenment and At-one-ment with the Divine Spirit.

This hierarchy is structured not only to provide balance and structure, but also to enable souls and spirits to express their free will and choice. You can choose to advance your soul and spirit through these levels, or you can choose to transgress so to speak and travel backwards as well.

From this approach, these are the Kingdoms that make up the "Divine Universe."

1. The Lower Kingdom

This is where the essence of negativity thrives. This lowest level of the Kingdom Hierarchy is reserved for souls who have created such evil and karma for their spirits that they have been banned by the Divine consciousness to their own realm of existence. People like Hitler, Saddam Hussein, Kim Jong-Il, and other such people who have committed "sins against humanity" would be the type of people relegated to this realm. This might included mass murders and serial killers as well.

This realm might also be known as limbo, and sadly, it's the location for souls who take their own lives. Suicide isn't just a 'sin' in non-pagan beliefs such as Christianity. From a metaphysical point of view, it's the ultimate contract breach and highest form of transgression against the spirit as well.

Remember, when your spirit is creating its blueprint, it is making agreements with other souls for karma, lessons, and events that will progress the evolution of both or all parties concerned. By ending those agreements abruptly through suicide, a soul is taking away those agreements that may have been desperately needed by the other party in order to advance their spirit. Everything is connected and interconnected in the Divine Universe. No one person is an island unto them self. And this is abundantly clear in situations like this.

This is also the realm of the mythological Demons. This is a group of angels or spirits who have been assigned to the negative ethers as a service to the Divine Universe. They inhabit this lower energy realm to assist with the "punishment" of condemned souls. Sadly, propaganda and entertaining stories depict these negative beings as having the capability to play havoc with unsuspecting incarnated souls. Many believe that "soul possession" by these Demon spirits continue even today.

From a metaphysical perspective, the Divine Spirit maintains balance through the Divine Universe by keeping a barrier between this realm and the upper six realms or levels of enlightenment. It would be pointless to condemn a soul to this lower kingdom only to provide an avenue where they could continue to torture and manipulate others in the upper kingdoms. Consequently, the Demon Angels maintain control in this realm, not just for the sake of the upper levels, but also for the varying souls in this realm as well. Segregating the souls existing in limbo from the souls of destruction is one method of maintaining Divine control and balance.

2. The Physical Kingdom

Where we as incarnated beings exist. Don't limit this realm to just Earth. Putting this realm just above the Lower Kingdom doesn't mean this is a negative or lowly place to be. It simply means that here on the physical realm, we are segregated from the Universal knowledge of our greater Spirit.

This segregation provides us with an opportunity to learn in what some call the Veil of Forgetfulness. We have the ability to look through the veil by looking within our soul and learning about our spiritual connection to the Divine Universe. If we choose not to look, then we might not advance as far or as quickly as we might like, but we can and often do still move our spirit forward.

Life is forever changing. It cannot be stopped, but some do feel a need to fight against change. This slows down the progression of knowledge and wisdom, which will affect the evolution of the soul toward enlightenment.

3. The "Earth bound" Kingdom

Where ghosts exist. We'll talk more about them later, but this is the realm of unresolved physical desires or events. The souls that reside here are not negative by nature. Many simply don't realize they have crossed over, they don't want to be dead, or their death happened so quickly that they feel they have unresolved issues to attend to.

4. The Animal Kingdom

Where nature thrives in spirit. Some religious paths believe humans can incarnate into animals and animals can incarnate into humans. Within these religious beliefs, this realm does not exist. Pagan Metaphysical beliefs state animals incarnate into other animals, and people into other people, but neither can incarnate across these lines.

You might think of this as "Doggie and Kitty Heaven" for instance. The hypothesis for this realm states that: Angels govern the Spirit of Nature. These Angels assist animal spirits to come and go through this Kingdom, but they assist in ascertaining if an animal has progressed through its life toward enlightenment as well. So animals can also progress to the kingdom of the Divine, just as we "humans" can. This belief further states that as a spirit of nature evolves and becomes more enlightened, it can choose to incarnate as a human or progress and move on to the Kingdom of the Divine.

Some also believe this is the realm of fairies, forest sprites and other such magickal folk. It is considered to be the kingdom for all of nature's innocent spirits, which would include plants as well as animals. Ever think about what happens to an Oak tree when it dies? Many believe plants and especially trees have a spirit within them. If that's true, then where does that spirit go once it has lived its life, or it has been cut down? Many believe it is to this kingdom of nature that those spirits cross over to.

5. The Spirit Kingdom

This is where our Spirit exists in ethereal form. It can be viewed as Summerland, Valhalla, the Otherworld, and a variety of other heavenly labels.

When our soul leaves the physical body and travels back to the larger spirit of ourselves, it is to this kingdom that we come to. On this level, we evaluate our physical life, what we learned, and what still may need to be done. This is the realm of our Spirit Guides, and where we can tap into spiritual knowledge and insight.

Here, our Spirit has access to all knowledge from the past, the future, and right now. There are no barriers to sight or understanding. All things are clear and can be answered from this realm.

6. The Angelic Kingdom

"The keepers of the Divine Universe," and the buffer between the intense Divine energy and the remaining spiritual realms. Many believe the Beings on this level have never been incarnated and act as the keepers of balance within the entire Divine Universe. They maintain control between the Kingdoms and guard the gates so to speak, assisting those who are ready to progress to At-one-ment with the greater Divine Spirit, or baring those who are not.

Some call this the realm of the Arch Angels who are at the top of the Angelic Hierarchy. The lower choirs of the Angelic Hierarchy maintain the balance within the lower kingdoms. Those lower choirs are themselves governed by the Archangels of this higher kingdom.

7. The Divine Kingdom

The realm of pure energy and Divine existence resides here. This is where the Great Spirits exist, "The God Level." The place that is oftentimes called, Seventh Heaven.

Even in this hierarchy you can see how someone might interpret the top realm as Heaven and the bottom as Hell. But the connotations of what those two places mean in our society today do not fit in this metaphysical concept. The Divine Kingdom isn't a place you can get into just by dying after living a good life. And the Lower negative Kingdom isn't a place you go just because you've transgressed in your past lifetime.

The most important thing to remember about the Seven Kingdoms of Spirit is that there is a conscious structure and hierarchy to their existence. That structure is designed to maintain balance within the Divine Universe as a whole. There are checks and balances as well as Divine Laws that are in place to maintain this balance. Keepers of those Laws, the Archangels, oversee the adherence to those laws and the balance between each Kingdom.

Navigating the Kingdoms of Spirit

Through enlightenment, we progress through the stages of spirit until we reach a state of divine choice. The choice is pretty simple, we can chose to incarnate again for the purpose of teaching others, or we can chose to move on to the next level and enter the Divine realm. There are those who don't believe Jesus was the "son of God" but rather a soul that chose to return to physical form to teach Divinity to others. And upon his death, his spirit moved to the Divine Realm. The same can be said for Buddha and Krishna as well.

But within most of these ideas, there is a belief that spirits never move into the Angelic Realm. The beings on this angelic level assist spirits to move between the lower realms, keeping order within the Divine universe. They also assist spirits to move from the Spirit Realm to the Divine Realm when the requirements of spiritual enlightenment have been reached.

The Sub-Levels of Spirit

Another component to this Pagan Metaphysical approach is that each Kingdom of spirit has several layers of knowledge. These Seven Planes of Wisdom must be traversed before a spirit is given a choice to return to physical form or progress to the Divine Consciousness. These Seven Planes of Wisdom even exist within the Angelic Kingdom, which are described as the Angelic Hierarchies and Choirs.

These sub-levels of spiritual existence are similar to states of awareness or stages of evolution. Once again it is a hierarchy of being. This concept is designed to maintain order and structure throughout the Divine Universe and within each Kingdom of spirit.

Progress made upon the Seven Planes of Wisdom is not specific to any one religion. A person can be a devout Christian and progress through these levels, just as a person who is Metaphysical or Pagan. Being connected to the greater Divine Spirit doesn't mean connected with the beliefs and understandings of Pagan Metaphysical thought or the specific doctrine of any one religion. The same connection can be acquired through any form of religious practice that promotes harmony, inner awareness, and respect for all things.

As an example, let's take a walk through the evolution of a spiritual being.

1. Basic essence of life takes place in the form of pure energy.

2. A corporeal physical being evolves.

3. The evolution to a Humanoid essence takes place.

4. Spiritual essence – Here, a person has a spiritual understanding, but may not "feel" the connection to the Divine. They tend to be followers of a religion, going through the motions because that's what they are "supposed" to do.

5. Spiritual Awakening – Searching for "who you are" as a spiritual being. Here, a person thinks for them self. They are looking for that inner connection to the Divine Universe.

6. Spiritual Awareness – At one with the Divine self and teaching others. Here a person may still have karmic issues to resolve and lessons to learn. But their previous incarnations have brought them to this higher level of spiritual awareness where they are no longer searching, but rather they have found their spirit and they are at one with their connection to the great Divine Spirit.

7. Divine Connection – Spiritually aware and connected to the great Divine Spirit in all aspects of life. This is the level of Buddha, Jesus, and others like them.

These levels do not imply that a person goes through one lifetime on that sub-level and then automatically progresses to the next level. An individual spirit might incarnate several times on level 5, before moving to the next sub-level. A spirit can also move backward based on their actions and karma. That doesn't mean they become an amoeba, but their level of understanding about whom and what they are diminishes. Please don't make the assumption that those with mental disease or handicaps are these kinds of people. It's not the same thing.

Many religions and belief systems have some form of evolutionary enlightenment concepts. Buddhists, Hindu, Native Americans, European Shamanism, and many others share these ideas. Each one, however, puts them into practice and belief in varying ways. In theory, even non-pagan beliefs have a form of this theory. If you're evil in life, you're sent to Hell; if you're not, you're sent to Heaven where your deeds are reviewed before you enter the Gates of Heaven.

Anatomy of the Soul

Spiritual and Physical DNA

What Is the Spirit?

The spirit is the culmination of all our lifetimes, experiences, energies, and spiritual essence from the beginning of creation to today. Every life, every memory, and every action ever taken on one's path, either in spirit or in the physical form, is the essence of a spirit. The whole of "who we are" lies within the greater part of ourselves in the Spiritual being or what some like to call the Holistic Spirit (the whole being).

Physical and Spiritual DNA

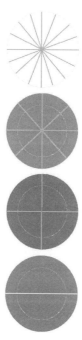

Human Genome

Upper Chakra System

Another way of saying this is that the Spirit is the form of pure energy, holding within it all the knowledge, wisdom, and experiences of that being. It is the being that holds the pure connection to the Cosmic Consciousness within the Divine Universe.

What Is the Soul?

The soul is a subset or smaller selection of our individual Holistic Spirit. This is the portion of our Spirit that we chose to pull into a single physical incarnation to work with and work on in a physical lifetime. Of all the lifetimes we've had, we couldn't cram all of the karmic debt/assets, knowledge, talents, or lessons into one physical incarnation. It would be overwhelming and too much to work on in one life. A physical human would simply feel scattered, unorganized, and simply wouldn't know where to start or how to do it. There would be too much information to choose from—we'd feel overcome and lost.

If there's one thing we know about the Divine existence, it's that the Universe is about balance. While in the form of our Holistic Spirit, we review all the knowledge and talents we've attained and determine what lessons and experiences we need to work on in the upcoming incarnation to grow and advance our evolution toward enlightenment. This is the first stage of our Spiritual Blueprint. This blueprint holds a general design of what we will need to face in the physical life in order to provide opportunities for spiritual learning, repaying or collecting karma, and the general mission of our lifetime.

Next, our Holistic Spirit chooses a maximum of twenty-two past lives to provide existing knowledge, talents, and instincts that will aid the incarnated person to accomplishing the goals set forth in the blueprint. These twenty-two past lives, and the upcoming incarnation (totaling twenty-three), create the Spiritual DNA of our physical being and the soul of the incarnated body.

So the spirit is the whole of who we are, the soul is a subset and what we are while in the physical body.

The composition of who we are, the color of our eyes, skin tone, hair color, family genetics, and so on are wrapped in the physical DNA we get from our parents. The twenty-three physical DNA compositions balanced with the twenty-three spiritual DNA compositions, make us who we are in mind/body/spirit. The two DNA bodies together, make us who we are in this lifetime.

Our soul is always connected to our larger spiritual body. This connection is maintained through what some call a "cord of energy." Some people describe this as a silver cord that travels from the solar plexus chakra within our body to the Holistic Spirit. This cord is always intact and is only broken when the physical body dies and our soul moves back to merge with the Holistic Spirit on the ethereal realm.

What Is Included in the Spiritual DNA?

Other than the karma brought forth from those twenty-two past lives, we pull in characteristics to define our spiritual purpose or goals in this new physical incarnation. These seven layers or seven spiritual characteristics help to create our foundation as an incarnated being. All these characteristics are combined with the physical DNA and help to make you the person you are today.

- Our Origin/Purpose (a mission so to speak like that of the Pleiadian bridge builder),
- Our Talents (such as communication),
- Our Skills (such as a skilled sculptor or gifted psychic),
- Our Environment (issues associated with living in a big family or an only child for instance),
- Our Background or Creed (such as being Irish),
- Our Potential (such as spiritual awareness),
- Our Spiritual Balance (such as incarnating as a female when most of your previous lives have been male).

What Are the Details of the Spiritual Blueprint?

As mentioned, the Holistic Spirit reviews its past incarnations, knowledge, karma, and stage of enlightenment and then makes a few decisions. The Spirit decides which past lives to pull into this one. What spiritual and physical lessons need to be worked on and learned? What are the karmic events that can be drawn from to aid in these lessons? The Holistic Spirit reviews all the past lives and decides which ones will be most beneficial to achieving those lessons. For instance, if the Spirit sees a need to learn compassion, it may choose from a lifetime where the soul was in the medical field. If the lesson is to learn self-confidence, but with an ounce of humility, it may choose a lifetime where the soul was a teacher, or an actor, or some equivalent profession. The key is choosing lifetimes that provide inner knowledge and wisdom that can be applied to the lessons the Holistic Spirit wants to learn for spiritual advancement.

At this same time, the Holistic Spirit will make agreements with other Spirits to join together in the coming life to resolve personal karma. This may include karma such as that between your mother and father, your friends, or who you will have opportunities with in the frame of intimate relationships. None of these agreements are preordained and set in stone. They are merely agreements to cross paths, share energy and provide potential opportunities for learning and working on mutual karmic lessons.

As with any blue print, as you build the structure, issues or situations arise that cause you to alter choices or to further detail or refine the original plan. In metaphysical terms, this is accomplished through the Law of Free Will and Choice. Through this Law we progress and evolve the soul by how we put our choices into action. Our Holistic Spirit can provide the situations, but the final outcome is never predefined. That is determined by free will and choice of the individual soul as an incarnated physical being. The fate you make as an incarnated being in the physical form will impact the Spiritual Blueprint and affect the overall choices made by the Holistic Spirit.

Because of this, the Spiritual Blueprint is immense, expansive, and detailed. It accounts for which path you take when confronted with a decision and the consequences of those choices. For instance, you may be presented with an opportunity to move to Africa and take your dream job. Your choice to accept the opportunity or not will have its own set of consequences. You will meet entirely different people if you go, or if you stay. Therefore, your blueprint will account for both avenues of the choice and adjust future opportunities accordingly.

Another example; some soul connection agreements made while in the Holistic Spirit will not be carried out, while others will. The Holistic Spirit makes several agreements with other Spirits to establish romantic partnerships in the next life. If this choice is made, agreement 1 is carried out and the other agreements are dropped. Or if that choice is made, agreement 1 never presents itself and agreement 2 occurs, results in a divorce and agreement 3 is carried out.

Free will and choice is forever changing and moving the energy and opportunities of your life. And the Spiritual Blueprint has been designed to keep up with those changes, providing new avenues and opportunities, which will require new choices and the continued exercise of your free will.

When The Soul Completes Its Mission

Once the soul has made its choices and completed its mission, it will leave this physical world. It's important to remember that the soul is always connected to the larger Holistic Spirit. At some point, the soul will see the life it has built and decide the construction has been completed. When the physical body dies, the soul detaches itself, the silver cord is broken and the soul prepares to return to the larger spiritual body. It takes with it the knowledge and wisdom from these new experiences that will be merged back into the Holistic Spiritual self.

Immediately after death, the soul will remain with the physical body until it is properly put to rest, if that's possible. Of course, there situations where that may not be possible, such as in times of war, floods, or other natural disasters or violent deaths. In these cases, the soul makes its own determination of when to leave the side of the physical body.

The soul will comfort those who mourn their passing and take the opportunity to say good-bye to those who were in their life. Typically, this occurs through dreams, but when a person has a talent of communication with spirit, the soul might make direct contact to say goodbye. There are millions upon millions of family legends, tales, and stories about a recently deceased relative being seen by a living member of the family to express their compassion and say good-bye. Or how many people do you know who have said their deceased Mother came to them in a dream the night of their death to say goodbye and let them know it was going to be okay?

When the physical connections have been put to rest, the soul will travel to the spiritual realm. That can be Heaven, Summerland, Valhalla, the Ethereal or Divine Energy plane of existence or a myriad of other spiritual locations. There are way too many hypotheses about what this spiritual place is to document here, even in the metaphysical world. So let's focus on what happens once your soul is in the spiritual realm.

Many people who have had near-death experiences have reported seeing a brilliant white light upon completing their mission here in the physical. They felt drawn to this light, and within it, they have seen their loved ones who had crossed over before them. Channeled information has supported this experience and explains that a soul is greeted into the spiritual realm by the souls of their loved ones. They will appear in forms that your soul will recognize and are familiar with, in order to ease your concern or fear and your journey into spirit.

The movie *Ghost* gave a wonderful example of this when Sam completed his mission on the physical plane and found his killer. He said goodbye to his wife and his friend; then the white divine light appeared before him. As he moved toward the light, those spirits he once knew greeted him and the gateway closed behind him.

The soul spends some time readjusting, at which time it rejoins the energy of the larger Holistic Spirit it came from. The knowledge, wisdom, and physical experience the soul gained while incarnated is now merged with the Holistic Spirit.

Divine energies and the Holistic Spirit make an assessment of growth. They review the progression of enlightenment based on the lessons in the past incarnation, karmic debt, and the future need for additional learning either while in spirit or through another incarnation. In other words, the Holistic Spirit determines what it learned and what it needs to repeat. What karma it repaid and what it gained, and so on. The Holistic Spirit now decides how to proceed on its path to At-one-ment.

There are many hypotheses about how long this takes. Those who believe in Rebirth, see the reincarnation of a soul as an instantaneous act from death to rebirth. Some cultures believe the death of a relative indicates a new child is to be born into that family as the soul leaves one existence and enters a new one within that same family. In theory, a grandfather who passes, could become his own great grandson.

In many Metaphysical communities, the progression is defined in somewhat open terms. The spirit remains in the spiritual realm for fifty years or more. Time does not flow on the spiritual realm the way we think of it here in our incarnated state. So "timing" of transitions is not set in stone and vary based on the choices of the spirit. Many spirits decide to provide service to other spirits it had been linked with. Such as taking on the role of Spirit Guide, for a soul who is still incarnated in the physical world. Your grandmother can become your relative guide. Your sister from a previous lifetime can become your spirit guide.

When the spirit has completed its work on the spiritual realm and decides to incarnate into another physical form, the whole process of building a new spiritual blueprint starts over again. When the Holistic Spirit achieves enlightenment, it is given the choice to return as a Master Teacher, such as Buddha or Jesus. Or it can choose to progress and become one with the Divine Consciousness. Now, at this stage, there are again many hypotheses for what occurs.

Some people believe the Holistic Spirit merges into a greater form of Energy Being. Others believe the Spirit moves onto another plane or realm of existence. Of course others believe the Spirit moves into Heaven or some other form of Divine existence. The possibilities are endless, and so are the beliefs associated with them. The bottom line is that no one truly knows for sure. But that's the basis of faith. What you believe and feel within yourself is the most important answer on your spiritual blueprint.

Kundalini

Kundalini is a Sanskrit word meaning to coil or spiral. It may also be known as Ki, Ch'i, Sushumna, Life Force energy, prana and varying other cultural-based names.

Kundalini energy is a vital flow of intelligent cosmic energy through the chakra system, linking the physical being with the greater cosmic spirit. It is also thought of as electromagnetic energy that stimulates the chakra centers along the spine and the endocrine system. This energy flows in a clockwise motion from the root chakra at the base of the spine to the crown chakra at the top of the head, and back to the root again. Kundalini energy flows continuously to stimulate each chakra point as it matures and opens within the soul.

The Flow of Kundalini Energy

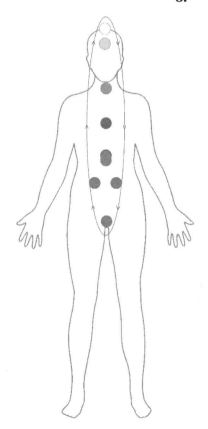

The concept is generally associated to Hindu and Yogic practices. But it's important to note that this concept of vital life force energy is by no means unique. It can be found throughout the world under varying names and labels. Scholarly debate sometimes dismisses other concepts or variations in Kundalini concepts because of the historical lineage between the word and yogic philosophies. I personally find that to be shortsighted. While other cultures may not have used the exact word *Kundalini,* the concepts are generally the same. As modern spiritual philosophies have emerged, a common language has also developed even if the concepts behind that language are more widely perceived. So you can call this energy what you choose, but for the sake of clarity and conversation, we'll call it Kundalini.

In yogic philosophy of ancient India, Kundalini is the mothering intelligence behind the awakening of spiritual maturity. This approach explains that Kundalini awakening is linked to the manifestation of "bio-energetic" energy. The appearance of this energy is also called the "pranic awakening." Prana is considered to be the vital and life-sustaining energy within the physical and spiritual body.

Kundalini energy can also be linked to the Chinese concept of Ch'i. This, too, is defined as the vital life force of the body. In this case, Ch'i is part of the air and taken in by breathing. It circulates through the body and makes up the twelve meridian lines within the body.

In Japan, this vital life force is called Ki. It can be found in the Christian Bible and the Rosicrucian order as "the divine universal essence pervading all nature; even unconsciousness and matter."

While many schools believe activation of the chakra centers occurs all at one time, other spiritual schools believe that activation occurs one chakra at a time. This perspective also suggests that specific types of energy and other vibrations, such as sound and words, can also stimulate these major chakra centers. Edgar Cayce prophesied that by saying the Lord's Prayer to stimulate the inner Divine life-force energy, all the chakras could be opened successfully for work.

In Tibetan and Indo-European Shamanistic teachings, the life-force energy flows through all energy centers, but may not open them until the individual is ready to work on the lessons and karmic issues governed by that energy vortex. This perspective follows a concept of right time, right place, and right energy.

Another school of thought suggests that Kundalini is the vital flow of Divine Energy within the physical body, connecting the soul to both the physical incarnation and the cosmic Holistic Spirit. This connection occurs from the moment a soul is created, and begins with energy flowing into the body from the Earth through the feet, along the spinal column and out the top of the head through the silver cord to the Holistic Spirit. Additionally in this hypothesis, it's not Kundalini that stimulates the chakras, but rather the energy of the chakras that feed the flow of the Kundalini Energy.

While there isn't complete agreement on the how and where this life-force energy comes from or enters the body, there is agreement on the why. As wisdom is learned, this electromagnetic energy continuously moves through the body along the spine, directed by the soul mind, as the soul mind meets the requirements of each Chakra and begins spiritual work.

In order for the soul to begin its work on karma or spiritual lessons, the chakra that is in line or associated with that spiritual energy must also be opened and ready to join in the process for work. Kundalini stimulates the chakra center and helps prepare the point to open and release the karmic energy held within it.

For instance, to work on intimate relationships on a spiritual and karmic level, the root chakra needs to be matured and open for expressing this type of sexual energy.

There are exceptions, for karmic reasons of course, but for most people, Kundalini isn't ready to open all the chakra centers until the physical body has developed and progressed to the point of puberty.

As lessons are learned and karma is processed, Kundalini energy moves up through the chakra stem, through the crown chakra to unite with the Silver cord and ascends to the higher realms of spirit.

Total activation of the chakras through Kundalini is said to bring total mental enlightenment. Through this enlightenment, the need for death and rebirth is no longer necessary, which means the individual spirit has achieved total enlightenment and oneness with the Universal Divine Spirit. Reincarnation then becomes unnecessary, unless the spirit desires to do so. But at this time, it's a matter of choice.

This path to Divinity may take many lifetimes to achieve. But in each lifetime an individual follows this basic plan:

The Basic Plan

Birth	Choosing karmic and spiritual lessons to be worked on in the physical embodiment
Kundalini Opens	The chakras are activated and opened
Trauma/Drama	The soul goes through karmic issues to receive or repay debts. At the same time, the soul goes through opportunities of learning spiritual lessons to advance the knowledge and wisdom of the soul.
Accepting the Cosmic Consciousness	Acknowledgement, Acceptance and Action
Divinity	Achieving At-one-ment

Chakras

Chakra is another Sanskrit term, which means wheel or disk. Also called meridians, energy centers, energy vortices, soul centers, in biblical terms they can be referred to as the Seven Stars and Seven Churches.

The concept of these energy centers has been around for a very long time and throughout the world and varying cultures.

The Chakra System

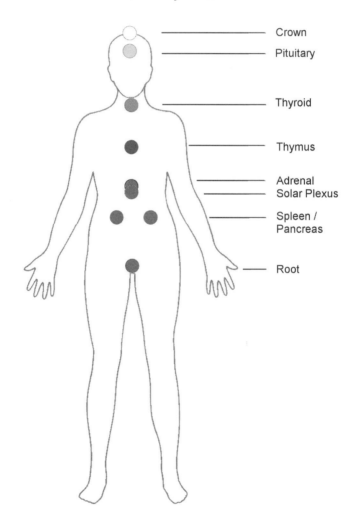

Chakras are the energy vortices at a sub-atomic level within your spiritual body. The complete system is the physical manifestation of the soul in the physical body. Simply put, the Chakras are the Soul in physical form. They hold the spiritual DNA, which includes the trace memories from past lives, the wisdoms and talents from past lives, the karmic debts and credits brought into this incarnation, and they act as the input centers for the cells of the body.

There are varying schools of thought about how many centers there are within the body, and the exact placement of these centers. The ancient Hindu texts of knowledge known as the *Vedas*, the *Tantra* and *Hatha* Yoga systems each indicate seven major centers within the body.

The Tantric Buddhists (the Vajrayana) have a different system than the Indian Tantric system. The Tantric Buddhist system focuses on four main energy centers (the navel, throat, heart, and head) but still recognize seven main chakra centers, with corresponding spokes radiating from each center.

Over 5,000 years ago, the Chinese discovered and identified twelve acupuncture meridians along which subtle energy travels in the human body. Meridians are the pathways of the positive and negative energy power, which carries on some of the communication between the various parts of human beings. Some people point to this system as one of the oldest concepts of chakras or energy vortices. But Eastern practices are not the only systems which recognized these energy centers.

Old Shamanistic cultures also recognized energy centers within the body. In Norse mythology, the ash tree Yggdrasill is said to be the tree of knowledge. It is the tree from which Odin is said to have hung from to gain enlightenment. Known as the World Tree, the knowledge of Yggdrasill defines a hierarchical system of nine levels or centers of energy. The Norse greatly influenced the concepts of Western pagan mysteries and these concepts permeated Indo-European Shamanistic beliefs.

As stated by *The Pagan Path* (1995 Farrar, Farrar and Bone), "There is a common saying among occultists that you should not mix traditions, particularly the Western and Eastern mystery traditions. We would like to point out to people who feel that this system does not belong in Western Pagan practice, that if they look closely they will find that most of our traditions are of common Indo-European heritage." It is from this common heritage that the concepts of nine chakra centers grew. They can further be connected to Indo-European Shamanism through their alignment with the lunar calendar and the practices associated with Moon cycles. In a purely metaphysical perspective, the Chakras can also be associated and aligned to the physical body's endocrine system. It is this system of nine Chakra Centers that I will discuss in this section.

Each major center carries with it a special purpose, a specific energy, color, and vibration. These components – movement, color, and sound – are the characteristics of the chakra centers.

Where Are the Chakras?

The chakras can't be seen with the physical eyes, x-rays, MRIs, or radio scans. They are sub-atomic energy centers located along the spinal column of living beings. Each vortex carries a special energy level that causes the chakra to spin at varying speeds.

Most of the chakras spin in a clockwise direction. The slowest movement of spin is at the Root chakra. As you move up the body toward the head, the chakra centers begin to spin faster. The only centers that spin in a counter-clockwise motion are the Pancreas/Spleen chakras. Where as all the other chakras face forward like a round clock, the Pancreas/Spleen sit sideways in the body, almost like a barbell. This spinning movement gives each chakra its own unique energy signature, color, and vibration or sound.

These unique energy patterns provide the focus or purpose of the center within the body. For instance, when you are working on issues of choice, you're working with the Thyroid chakra. When you are working on matters of transformation within your life, you're working on the Solar Plexus center. By understanding this system of energy and their associated purpose, you can focus energy work within your being to areas that need assistance to open for improvement and work. You might even want to focus energy on specific areas for healing, to learn or let go and break old patterns that may be holding you back on both a spiritual and physical level.

The following is a brief overview of each center, its characteristics and its purpose within the body.

Pineal (Crown, 1st vortex)

Located at the top of the head. Also known as the "crown chakra" it represents the beginning. It is our connection to the cosmic consciousness or Universal Divine Spirit. The fastest spinning center, this chakra vibrates with the brightest light. The color that most describes this energy level is white.

Pituitary (2nd vortex)

Located between the brows, in the center of the forehead. Also known as the location of the "third eye," this chakra is considered to be the gateway to the higher self. Where you can send and receive your spiritual communications, or open to visually perceive spiritual energy. It reflects the oneness of spirit with the oneness of life. This chakra vibrates with a violet glow.

Thyroid (3rd vortex)

Located in the throat. This chakra represents the Will center. It is the coming together of the higher and lower chakras. It is the source where spiritual will blends with physical choices. This chakra vibrates with a blue glow.

Thymus or Heart (4th vortex)

Located in the center of the chest, next to the heart. Also called the heart chakra, it synthesizes the spiritual and physical natures in harmony and love. It is also known as the center of unconditional love. This chakra vibrates with a green glow.

Solar Plexus (5th vortex)

Located where the rib cage meets at the bottom. It represents the creative center, where transition takes form and shape. This center fosters the co-creation with the soul and helps the physical body manifest issues, situations, needs, and desires. This chakra vibrates with a bright yellow glow.

Adrenals (6th vortex)

Located just a little up and behind the solar plexus. This chakra represents the protection center. This is where the body holds onto the karmic lessons for this lifetime. This center vibrates with a yellow glow, surrounded with a green border.

Pancreas (7th vortex)

Located below and to the right of the solar plexus, this Pancreas chakra governs how we honor our physical kingdom. It helps us to maintain our physical nature in balance with our spiritual nature. It is the "as above, so below" center. This center vibrates with an orange glow, much like the color of a pumpkin.

Spleen (8th vortex)

Located below and to the left of the solar plexus, the Spleen chakra is the rejuvenation center. It helps the spiritual body heal itself after a karmic lesson has been successfully resolved, or when too much energy is put out to others or to a situation. Like the Pancreas center, this chakra vibrates with a pumpkin color. And these are the two centers that spin counter-clockwise within the body.

Root (9th vortex)

Located at the base of the spine, at the cervix. The last and slowest spinning chakra, this center governs security and the grounding of one's energies. It is the security of the soul in this embodiment for the guarantee of health and survival. This chakra center vibrates with a red glow.

When the Kundalini energy first opens the spiritual body, it begins here at the base in the root chakra. Because this center is located within the area of the reproductive organs, Kundalini will not open until these organs are fully functional. For children, this occurs at the time of puberty. A child could experience sever bouts of confusion, trauma, or even illness if the Kundalini opens too soon.

The upper chakras (from the solar plexus up) are the perennial chakras that progress through each physical embodiment. These are the constant centers of the soul within each embodiment. They hold the memories, the talents, and the past knowledge of all your previous lifetimes drawn into this physical existence.

The lower chakras are the annual centers. These chakras are re-created with each embodiment as they deal more with the matters of the physical being and the physical world. They contain the issues that the spirit has placed within the Spiritual Blueprint to work on in this lifetime. They are called the physical chakras for this reason.

What Do Chakras Do?

As we progress through this embodiment, the lessons and energy we experience on a day-to-day basis will stimulate a particular chakra center. The chakras affect the regulatory flow of energy, which results in affecting of the physical body. Or simply put, the chakra's energy manifests in the body when we're working on issues that relate to the purpose or function of that chakra. This could manifest in a desire, a certain way of looking at something, an instinct that influences a reaction to a situation, or our ability to recognize opportunities and to act upon them.

For instance:

If you're working on matters of "will," such as choosing not to stand up for yourself and speak your mind, then you may experience disturbances in your throat. If you are constantly holding back how you feel, or how you WANT to express yourself, you may develop a sore throat. The longer you ignore the lessons brought to you by this energy vortex, the more severe the disturbance in the physical body will become. The sore throat turns into strep throat and the progression continues until you resolve the underlying issue.

When you learn the positive force of the lessons you experience and can move the soul forward, the energy of the chakra works with you instead of against you. A person who can speak their will, without negative reaction, can become a wondrous singer for instance.

Exercise: Energize the Chakras

Take time to focus on your chakras, open them for spiritual work and become in-tune with your own energies.

1. Close your eyes and take in a deep breath.

2. Relax and let your stress and anxiety leave your body. With each exhale see your stress move out of your presence like a gray smoke, traveling out into the ethers where it will be dissipated and no longer do harm to anyone.

3. Take in another deep breath and feel yourself begin to relax. One more deep breath and imagine the white light of Divine energy coming in through your nose and pushing out the remaining stress and negativity.

4. Move your focus to your solar plexus and see a relaxing Divine white light growing within your being. As you return to normal breathing, imagine the light expanding until your entire body is engulfed in white light.

5. Picture this light pushing out any left-over negativity, stress or anxiety and know the Divine Universe is working with you to set a shield of protection around you, keeping you safe and secure. As if you were in the palms of the Divine Spirit.

6. Now move your focus to the root chakra. Imagine it's deep dark red color, spinning clockwise, very slowly.

7. Visualize the white light move into the spinning circle. Making the dark red color glow in a clear and vibrant manner. As if you were looking through a colored piece of dark red glass. No flaws, no fog or smoke. Just clear vibrant light. Imagine the white divine light energizing this center in a manner that brings peace and serenity to the area. Think of this like turning a flash light on, inside the spinning vortex. Allow the Divine light to flow into this center stimulating the energy to ground and become secure within its circular movement.

8. Move the light upward to the Pancreas and Spleen chakras. Visualize the white light moving into these pumpkin colored centers. Imagine these two centers slowly turning in a counter-clockwise motion. See the Divine Light infusing these centers with balance of spirit and body. Helping to open the rejuvenation and healing properties contained within these areas to bring about health and vitalization within your spiritual and physical being.

9. Progress upward to the Solar Plexus chakra center. Picture its yellow light gently spinning a little faster than the previous chakras in a clockwise manner. Visualize the white light moving into the center of this chakra and revitalizing it with Divine energy. Fostering its co-creation with the soul and the physical body, in order to assist you in creating your goals, dreams, and spiritual mission. You can because you are one with the unlimited power of Divine Spirit's energy of creation.

10. Travel upward to the Adrenal chakra. Watch the white light gently move into this area and see it caress the green outer layer and softly move into the yellow center. Imagine the Divine light empowering the entire center, as it spins in a clear and crisp color of yellow and green. Stimulating its power of protection within you and around your physical body.

11. Step upward to the Thymus/Heart Chakra. Watch the Divine white light enter its beautiful crystal clear green energy center. Notice the quickened speed of its spin and the calmness surrounding it as the Divine Light energizes this area releasing compassion and love of self, along with acceptance and tolerance for all those around you and throughout the world.

12. Move upward to the Thyroid/Throat chakra and see its fast clockwise blue spinning vortex. Imagine the Divine Light entering this center, stimulating its energy, providing confidence, peace, and serenity to empower your will to succeed in all facets of your life. You can, because you are one with the Divine universe.

13. Progress upward to the Pituitary/3rd Eye chakra. Picture its purple glow spinning extremely fast as the Divine Light gently enters its circular body. See the light provide clarity to its vision of your being within and the world outside your physical body. Imagine yourself seeing the spiritual energy and lessons behind the situations in your life, giving you understanding of spirit and mission at the same instant.

14. Travel upward once more to the Crown Chakra. See the Divine Light merge into its very fast-paced movement. Imagine the Divine white light and the white energy of this chakra combining to caress each other, as if welcoming each other back home. See the Divine Light empowering this center with understanding and wisdom as it aids in opening a spiritual connection within your being, to your own inner Divine mind and that of the Divine Universal consciousness.

15. Finally picture the Divine white energy gently traveling down to the Root chakra, caressing each vortex as it travels along your spine. Imagine the energy traveling effortlessly back up through each chakra center as it progresses in a clockwise manner up to the Crown and back to the Root, repeating its pattern continuously.

16. As you leave this visualization in motion, slowly begin to feel this energy empowering your entire being. Leaving you feeling uplifted, secure, and ready to take on any issue or opportunity in your daily life.

17. Take in a deep breath and release any trepidation, stress, or anxiety you may have remaining within your being.

18. Open your eyes. Take a moment to feel the physical world around you and become cognoscente of your surroundings.

19. This ends the meditation.

It's a good idea after each exercise to record your thoughts and feelings related to what you just completed. Journaling not only documents your experience for future review, but it can also provide you with interesting information that you might not have picked up on while conducting the exercise. Don't second-guess what you write down, just let it flow through you. Don't forget to record the date, time, place, moon phase, and even the weather. All this can provide you with information later as you put patterns together and try to learn from them.

Chakra Center Map

The image of the Chakra System Movement and Function maps the placement of each energy vortices, its function, color, and movement. You can use this map to help visualize the centers during your meditations, for healing work, or to help decipher ailment messages as they occur.

The Chakra System Movement and Function

Movement	Chakra Description		Chakra Function	Color
Clockwise Fastest Spin	Pineal or Crown Spiritual Source		Divinity Source of Divine Consciousness Ultimate state of awareness	Bright White
Clockwise	Pituitary Gifts Of The Spirit		Perfected Humanity Oneness of Spirit to Oneness of Life Governs Wisdom, Knowledge & Channeling abilities	Violet
Clockwise	Thyroid Higher Purpose		Spiritual & Physical Nature The Balance Center Blends spiritual will with physical choices	Royal Blue
Clockwise	Thymus or Heart Unconditional Love		Physical Purpose As above, so below Governs the implementation of the Spiritual blue print	Emerald
Clockwise	Adrenal Master Of Physical Life		Spiritual Purpose Links the physical embodiment to the Spiritual blue print	Yellow with Green Border
Clockwise	Solar Plexus Creativity & Transfiguration		Manifestation & Transformation Promotes creation between the physical and the soul	Yellow
Counter-Clockwise	Pancreas / Spleen Spiritual Abundance		Physical Maintenance / Rejuvination Maintains the spiritual DNA within the physical	Pumpkin
Clockwise Slowest Spin	Root Spritual Grounder		Security Governs physical health, wellbeing and survival	Deep Red

The Conscious Minds

Spiritual Psychology

Spiritual Psychology is an understanding of humans being multi-layered entities with a Mind, Body, and Spirit according to author and teacher of energy medicine Donna Eden. Commonly known as integral, transpersonal, or spiritual psychology, this spiritual approach to the mind is a method that seeks to explore the full range of human potential in relationship to and with the spirit.

Dr. Michelle Lusson describes Spiritual Psychology as a method that seeks to understand the three layers of the human being. The person we display to the world, the person we see our self as, and the person we really are within our spiritual existence. This process of understanding helps an individual gain insight into the trials we feel that have moved us away from our spiritual path, created karma, and consequently caused us to feel separated from the Divine force within our life and our own Higher Self. We can let go of these pains and fears to gain understanding about the lessons our soul seeks to acquire and to see ourselves in a new light. This approach can bring about a holistic understanding of our whole being.

These layers of human consciousness are represented in the levels of being or the Mind, Body, and Spirit of an individual. Through an understanding of who we are at a sub-atomic level, we can begin to see how the layers of consciousness are developed, intertwined, and support or hold back the spiritual evolution of a person.

Mind, Body and Spirit

Everyone has heard about these bodies of existence known as the mind, body and spirit. But there are also corresponding conscious minds for each of these areas of an individual as well. In the simplest of terms, we are made up of four levels of being or consciousness.

1. The physical consciousness

The physical mind or body being

2. The soul consciousness

The soul mind or mind being

3. The spiritual consciousness

The spirit mind or spirit being

4. The Divine Consciousness

The Divine mind

We can see these in action when we look at the corresponding levels of consciousness within ourselves.

The Conscious Self: The Physical Mind

The physical brain is the mind of the Body. This is the individual's conscious mind, the part of the self that governs day-to-day activities. Where the individual reasons and processes information that interact with and where they hold their current life memories. This is the part of self that we display to the world around us.

The Higher Conscious Self: The Soul Mind

The sub-consciousness is the mind of the Soul. This area of being is also called the higher consciousness of the self. This is the part of the self that talks to an individual's conscious mind and represents the true self of a person. Being our spiritual presence in this incarnation, this is the part of self that we perceive ourselves to be.

If an individual is someone who holds a lot of doubts about who they are, those thoughts are held in the subconscious mind. No matter what the physical mind does, or tries to present to others, the energy behind the doubt is still held in the subconscious mind. This is one of the reasons that what an individual thinks of the self is so important to their overall health. To overcome obstacles, an individual must start with their subconscious mind.

The Super Conscious Self: The Spirit Mind

The super consciousness is the mind of the Spirit. This is where an individual holds the aspect of the Divine within them self. Some call this level of consciousness the Divine Self or the God-Self. You might think of this as the controlling mind of the whole being. This is where an individual holds all past life memories; it's their reasoning center for making choices on a spiritual level.

The Divine Consciousness: The Universal Connection

The Divine Spirit is "The Everything, The All" that exists. It's everything connected together throughout all of creation through energy. It is, for lack of a better word "God" and we are each part of and connected to that Divine consciousness. The Divine Conscious mind within an individual is the connection or bridge to the knowledge and energy of the greater Universal Divine Spirit.

Spiritual Psychology strives to help an individual discover the knowledge, wisdom, and the answers they hold within their levels of Consciousness. Not just to understand whom they are and why they are here, but also to help face the challenges of life. To discover understanding behind the issues or events that cross our path in order to address them and heal from them when appropriate.

From this perspective, handling day-to-day trials and tribulations can be learning lessons for the soul and provide experiences to evolve the spirit. Understanding the spiritual lesson, connections to other souls and higher Divine energy, to the karma behind an event can lessen the confusion and provide opportunities for learning. In very tough situations, it can ease the pain and help an individual heal from the grief associated with a hardship they have faced.

Building A Bridge Between Minds

Meditation is the way we build the bridge between each aspect of our conscious, super conscious and spiritual conscious minds. By making this connection stronger and stronger each time you meditate, you are establishing a permanent bridge between these levels of thought and existence. This allows you to communicate between each level of your being at any time of the day or night, instead of just during meditation or ritual work.

In establishing and maintaining this bridge, you are better able to view an issue, or problem from a higher perspective. Doing this can help you react to troubling situations in a positive light, instead of having a knee-jerk reaction. These negative instincts can often make matters worse. Along with prolonging a hardship or causing the soul to repeat the lesson over and over again either in the current embodiment or in a future incarnation.

This approach allows you to see if a situation is based on karma that you are trying to work on, a spiritual lesson placed on your Spiritual Blueprint, or if it's an opportunity to help someone else through the knowledge you have attained. After all, the phrase "we hurt the ones we love" isn't just a euphemism. We sometimes do this as a means to beg for help, lashing out at others as a reflection of what's hurting us inside our own being.

Having this level of inner communication helps you to "see" with your Divine Self, or another way to say it, with your Spiritual Eyes. You can tap into your Divine Self and guide your physical actions throughout your day. This helps people walk the path of their soul. It allows an individual to make choices during the day that can lead closer to fulfilling the purpose and mission of the soul and the intent of their life in this incarnation.

In addition to building a bridge through meditation, you also have the ability to affect the negative aspects of the self that you don't like. You can't correct a bad habit or a negative thought process when you aren't even aware of it or not willing to admit it to yourself. Setting this bridge in place opens a pathway between your physical mind and the higher levels of consciousness where you can communicate honestly with yourself. It provides you the insight and the strength to face your fears, alter your negative thoughts and doubts, and overcome destructive patterns that maybe the result of earlier trails in this life, or karmic issues from a past life.

When we can be honest with ourselves, we can consciously work to change the subconscious thought patterns that hold us back.

Exercise: Connection ConsciousnessMeditation

Some people like to decorate their meditative space with a spiritual symbol, a Celtic cross, Ankh, pentacle, or other symbols to add to the spiritual significance of this meditation.

Find a piece of music you really like for meditation and stick with it. If you use the same piece each time you meditate, you will pre-program your mind to step into a state of relaxation. Each time you practice, your mind will move into this state with less effort and more quickly, allowing you more time for greater meditative work. My personal favorite piece of music is called, "Ascension to All That Is" by Robert Slap.

1. Sit in a comfortable position, in a chair or on the floor. Make sure your back is straight and the position you choose will be relaxing for a ten to fifteen minute meditative session. Do not lie down! An upright position allows the positive energy to flow through you and assist in the process. It should also help you to not fall asleep.

2. Take a minute to relax and focus your energies. Close your eyes and visualize your hands lighting a white candle in the center of your lower chest. This is your solar plexus and the center of your being.

3. Take in three deep breaths through your nose and three exhales through your mouth. With each breath, imagine the positive white light of the Divine Universe entering your nose, energizing your lungs and gently feeding the flame of the internal candle. As you exhale through your mouth, imagine any negativity, stress, and anxiety exiting your body. Say to your self: "I release all stress and negative emotions to the universe from my body and my home, where it will be dissipated and no longer do harm to anyone." See the negative energy leaving your body like a gray smoke, traveling upward through the ceiling, through the roof and out into the depths of space where it dissipates and fades away.

4. Return to normal breathing and focus on the flame within your solar plexus. With each breath you take in, see this light growing, gently increasing and filling your body with Divine energy. Watch it fill up your body like a vessel holding positive white light within your being.

5. Now imagine a focused stream of this white light moving up your spine and into your physical mind. See this light gently moving in a clockwise motion, like a spiral swirling around your consciousness. Visualize the person you are out in the world; this is the being you present to those around you. As you hold this image, imagine the white divine light swirling through your consciousness and slowly changes to a vibrant pink glow of love. Imagine this pink light surrounding the person you have envisioned and hugging it.

6. As you maintain that feeling of self love, see the person you envisioned floating upward into your deeper consciousness to your sub-conscious/soul mind. See the physical person hugging the higher soul body of yourself. Picture your conscious body and your subconscious soul greeting each other and connecting to one another in harmony and peace through a mutual love and respect of self.

7. Create an image of these conscious bodies still connected traveling upward deeper into your super-conscious Divine Mind. This time, see your highest level of conscious opening its arms to welcome your conscious and sub-consciousness. As these bodies of energy touch, feel your connection to the greater Divine world lock into place. Imagine your spirit opening to the Divine energy of the Universe. Feel yourself connect to "God" and become one with all things seen and unseen through out all life.

8. Take a few moments to hold this image and feel the energy of the Divine Self permeate your subconscious and conscious minds. See this connection of all levels of your being becoming stronger and flowing with energy in a continuous clockwise circle of white and pink streams of light. See it as never fading, never dissipating, but always remaining strong and in motion.

9. Allow any images or messages of communication to come into your vision. If you don't understand the message, by all means ask questions. Try to state what you think the message is and allow it to change to clarify the answer. If you see no images or feel no messages, that's okay too. It's not common or expected. But it can happen, so if it does just take note.

10. When you're ready, allow the subconscious and conscious bodies to

float back to their levels of being. But as you depart each layer of consciousness, imagine a permanent cord of communication remaining between each spirit, mind, and body existence.

11. Slowly allow your conscious mind to come back into the room where you're sitting. Feel the chair and floor, feel the room around you, become aware of the subtle sounds and light in the room. When you're ready, open your eyes and take in a deep cleansing breath.

12. This ends the meditation.

Before you go about the remaining activities of the day, record your experience in as much detail as you can in your spiritual journal.

Karma

As mentioned earlier, karma is the result of previous acts or deeds, either in the recent past or in past lives. Many people, for some reason, think there is only "bad" karma. But think about it, if you owe karma to someone, then someone is in a position to receive a karmic repayment. So there is both positive and negative karma to balance out in any given lifetime.

There are a few laws to karma. *What you put out you get back*, and *what you sew so shall you reap* are old euphemisms that say the same thing. The negative karma you gain must be paid back or dealt with in this lifetime, or in the next life to correct the karma credit. The Lady Warrior, who conquers unjustly in one life, may have to face being conquered in later years of the same lifetime, or in a later incarnation.

The soul experiences this karmic effect until it can detach (*let go and let God*) from the past life. When this occurs the soul has reached atonement, or what many metaphysical practitioners like to call "At-one-ment." If the soul can't let go, it can rubber band itself back to the "conquered" life so to speak starting the lesson over again.

It's very important to learn how to accept, and let go. Not just how to pay back karma, but also how to receive karmic payment. Gloating about winning a situation can be just as damaging as being a sore loser. Even too much of a good thing can be bad when we're talking about karma.

Now how can you tell the difference between karma and a spiritual lesson? Both can come in the form of recurring patterns. But karmic situations (especially negative karma) cannot be avoided, and usually come with some degree of drama/trauma. These are the situations that give you physical, mental, and spiritual concern, stress, or grief.

A spiritual lesson is something you can choose to avoid. By making a choice you might alter a situation and take a different path to face a different lesson that you're ready to handle. Your Spiritual Blueprint, however, will find a way to bring you back to the same fork in the road to deal with the original lesson again. But just like all things, you have free will and choice and can once more choose to avoid the lesson.

You have to be a careful not to judge the karmic situation or the opportunity for a spiritual lesson from the surface of things.

Let's take an example.

Helen Keller came into a life where she was deaf, blind, and could not speak. This doesn't necessarily mean she was afflicted with negative karma or that she was being punished for some previous dastardly deed in a previous incarnation. It's easy for some to make that judgment.

But consider this: She may have chosen to be born with these traits in order to bring an important and revolutionary method of communication to others like her. Through the creation of Braille and the expansion of sign language, she brought the gift of communication to millions of people throughout the world. And that legacy continues today. So would you say her "affliction" was from a karmic debt? Or could it have been a gift of sacrifice that her soul took on, in order to serve humanity?

Releasing Karma

It is through the resolution of karma and attaining spiritual enlightenment that we travel the path to divinity. This is both repaying and receiving karmic debts or credits. As well as, the karmic situations our soul has taken on to learn lessons to advance our own spirit. Some think of this as karma of self.

The five steps to enlightenment outline the process our soul goes through to attain this knowledge.

1. We're born to the physical world.

2. Kundalini energy opens and prepares the soul for the work it came into this life to do.

3. Through physical actions and interactions with others, we repay our karmic debts, learn spiritual lessons, and advance the soul.

4. Accepting the Divine Consciousness within our being and accepting our connection to the Divine Universal Spirit, we learn to acknowledge, accept, take action, and release the negative. Establishing a positive or divine path for our Spirit to progress and evolve.

5. We transition to spirit and continue this pattern until we achieve At-One-Ment with the greater Divine Universal Spirit and attain total enlightenment.

This simple process can be achieved through work and conscious choices. It will not be achieved in a single lifetime. But with each progression of learning we can change how we react to others, approach situations with love and Divine energy, accept the past and let go of the negative, and walk the spiritual path with a sense of Divine Consciousness. All this is needed to progress the soul forward in each embodiment.

Changing Old Patterns
To Release Karma

Through the process of Acknowledgment, Acceptance, Forgiveness, and Action, you can work toward releasing old patterns. This process applies to just about every aspect of life. But it's especially important to spiritual growth and the evolution of the soul through each physical embodiment.

Acknowledgment

You can't work on a karmic issue, release an unwanted habit, or change a subconscious thought pattern until you know it exists or are willing to admit it exists. So you first have to acknowledge the situation within yourself on a conscious level.

Acceptance

Once you've faced the fact that the issue or pattern does exist, you must accept that it exists. And that, yes indeed, you have been acting in a destructive way toward yourself and/or others in your life. This is an exercise in unconditional love of the self. To accept the characteristic or actions without judgment and to just recognize it with love instead of condemnation.

Forgiveness

Now that you've accepted the pattern, give yourself a break and forgive yourself for taking on this mold of yourself. You're human and we all do things we wish we wouldn't do. No one expects you to be absolutely perfect. So don't expect that from yourself. It is what it is, you've acknowledged the pattern and you want to change it. There's no reason to feel regret or guilt about the issue now. You can't change the past or what has been done, but you can change the way you allow the past to control your present and affect your future. Focus on that and extend forgiveness to yourself and anyone else that might need it in this situation.

Action and Letting Go

Now the Action to correct these thought patterns, or repay this karmic debt, can be implemented. In affecting change in your life, you are letting go of the past and moving toward self-growth and enlightenment. Depending on what the karmic issue or pattern is will dictate the action you take. But the action should be positive and motivating in a positive way.

Until you're willing to be open and honest with yourself, you cannot change the negative or destructive circumstances that exist in your life whither they are karmic or not. It takes effort, will power, and the ability to learn to trust your self. You can do whatever you set your mind to do. You know a lot more than you give yourself credit for. It's just a matter of sitting down and looking in the mirror to say: "I love me and I'm worth the effort to be the person I desire to be."

Akashic Records

Akashic (Sanskrit akasha, "primary substance")

Going hand in hand with Karma and past-life incarnations are the Akashic Records. The Akasha as they are sometimes called, are the file cabinets of an individual's past lives and deeds. Think of these records as individual folders in a large file cabinet. Each folder holds a past life of the individual spirit. All these folders combined into one cabinet are your personal Akashic Records or Akashic library of your greater Spirit.

The folders within the cabinet hold the knowledge, talents, experiences, lessons learned, and karma received or gained from that lifetime. You can open a folder and look in a mirror, so to speak, at who you were 200 years ago and discover how that life is influencing this current incarnation. What talents or knowledge did you pull from that lifetime to assist with the mission of this lifetime? What karma did you pull from to work on today?

Contrary to popular belief, not everyone can tap into your Akashic records. These are extremely sacred folders that hold the very essence of who you are as a spiritual being and who you are as a physical human. The Divine Spirit places a great responsibility onto individuals who can tap into that information. These records are the most important piece of your spirit and soul. As such, access to them is granted to the person them self, and to a few talented channels who have proven to the greater Divine Spirit, their understanding and acceptance of the responsibility, even accountability of looking into these folders.

Even then, the only folders available to you in this incarnation are the twenty-two lifetimes you've chosen for your spiritual blueprint. While you may be able to see glimpses of the others, more detail about those will be fleeting. If you think about it, this makes sense. You have enough to work on and deal with for the missions you chose to face in this embodiment. Why cloud the issues by adding additional information that doesn't assist in that process?

In order for a gifted channel to attain the responsibility to review the Akasha of another being, he or she must prove their worthiness. This can be accomplished through the redemption of karma, learning their own spiritual lessons, advancing their soul through knowledge and wisdom, and attaining a certain level of enlightenment. It's vitally important for the general psychic to realize this.

A psychic can "pick-up" on the energies around a person that make up the essence of who that person is. But the details, the karmic lessons, and patterns that many try to interpret really can't be pinpointed without looking into the Akashic records. Those who try to provide interpretive information could be creating some very serious karma for themselves as well as the individual seeking their assistance. To manipulate a person's path or direction based on false information, even if it isn't intended, is a severe transgression in the spiritual realm.

Information of this type is considered sacred because of the level of understanding of self that it brings to the soul. An individual could make life-changing decisions based in part on what someone tells them they are intended to do in this life. If that information is not accurate, or clouded in some manner by the psychic, an individual could waste a great deal of time in walking the wrong path; or worse totally divert from their spiritual blueprint impacting the very reason they incarnated into this life to begin with.

Of course the individual has responsibility here as well. You have free will and choice to make the decisions that affect your life. Never should an individual make choices based solely upon the information received from a psychic. No matter how accurate or well respected that psychic is.

For the individual person, there are many ways one can use to tap into their own Akashic records. Meditation is one of the easiest and best methods. Other methods include creative visualization, past-life regression or dream therapy. The best thing to do is find out which method will work best for you. Though I highly recommend meditation, as this will provide benefits in many other areas of your life as well.

Spiritual Sanctuary

The best place to get started is by discovering your own Spiritual Sanctuary. A Spiritual Sanctuary is your place in the ethers (the divine realm) where you can go to learn about your own soul, discover answers to your spiritual questions, and perform spiritual work. It is a structure of any kind where you are protected, safe, and free to explore your own awareness without concern or judgment. It is the door way or some call it the library of your Akashic.

The structure of your sanctuary will tell you a lot about yourself—about how your past incarnations are affecting you in this lifetime including which lifetimes you feel the most connected to or perceive yourself to be from. The general design and decoration can display your inner view of your spiritual embodiment and in addition to giving you insight to who you are, it can also provide comfort and a sense of "home" within your life.

The structure size, description, and feel will all be a representation of that which you are now, and how you are connected to your spiritual past. So try not to go into a meditation to discover your Spiritual Sanctuary with any preconceived ideas. Just let the image come to you. And don't worry if you find it and over time it changes. It should change as you learn more about yourself, progress on your spiritual mission, and tap into additional elements of your past incarnations to face obstacles or opportunities in this embodiment. Life is ever flowing and ever moving in constant change. The spiritual environment around should also flow and change with that progression.

Exercise: Find Your Spiritual Sanctuary

Since this is a special meditation, you may want to prepare your meditation space in a special way. Add a few ritualistic events, such as lighting a white candle and saying a prayer stating your intent for this meditative session. Some people like to decorate their meditative space with a spiritual symbol, a Celtic cross, Ankh, pentacle, or other symbols to add to the spiritual significance of this meditation. Take your time; try to imagine as much detail as possible.

1. Sit in a comfortable position, in a chair or on the floor. Make sure your back is straight and the position you choose will be relaxing for a ten to fifteen minute meditative session. Do not lie down! An upright position allows the positive energy to flow through you and assist in the process. It should also keep you from falling asleep.

2. Take a minute to relax and focus your energies. Close your eyes and visualize your hands lighting a white candle in the center of your lower chest. This is your solar plexus and the center of your being.

3. Take in three deep breaths through your nose and three exhales through your mouth. With each breath, imagine the positive white light of the Divine Universe entering your nose, energizing your lungs, and gently feeding the flame of the internal candle. As you exhale through your mouth, imagine any negativity, stress and anxiety exiting your body. Say to your self: "I release all stress and negative emotions to the universe from my body and my home, where it will be dissipated and no longer do harm to anyone." See the negative energy leaving your body like a gray smoke, traveling upward through the ceiling, through the roof and out into the depths of space where it dissipates and fades away.

4. Return to normal breathing and focus on the flame within your solar plexus. With each breath you take in, see this light growing, gently increasing and filling your body with Divine energy. Watch it fill up your body like a vessel holding positive white light within your being.

5. Say a prayer asking the Divine for guidance and help with the purpose of this mediation to discover your Spiritual Sanctuary.

6. This step takes a little practice, don't worry if you can't do this for any extended period of time, but at least give it a try. Keep your eyes closed, but look up at the pituitary gland. This is your brow chakra, where the third eye is located. Try to keep your eyes focused on this point. The muscles around your eyes may become sore as you stretch them upward, so don't over do this at first. As you practice your spiritual meditations, this step will become easier and easier to do.

7. As you focus on your third eye imagine you're at the base of a staircase, dimly lit, but inviting. Imagine your soul body standing up from your physical body seated in its meditative place. Envision yourself walking toward the staircase and moving up each step. See the lights on the walls and the texture of the floor as you progress upward.

8. Picture just a head of you, about ten yards, you see a set of glass doors and through those doors you can see a brilliant white light. You feel in your heart that this is the light of the universal consciousness, of the Divine. A feeling of Peace, calm, protection, and knowledge fills your insides. With each step closer, you feel more relaxed and at peace, you feel uplifted and connected to this universal energy.

9. As you approach the doors, they automatically open and invite your soul into this realm of enlightenment. As you pass through, you can see a beautiful structure waiting for you. Take note of what the structure is, this is your Spiritual Sanctuary. Try to notice as much detail as you can about its outside and make mental notes of it. Decipher what's around the structure, where it's located and what is present in the general area.

10. See yourself moving closer to the structure. As you do, take note of any additional details and features more clearly. Within a moment, you are at the entryway, what does it look like? As you study the entry it opens and welcomes you inside.

11. Imagine yourself walking inside and take some time to look around. Try to take notice of all things in the sanctuary. Walk to the center and sit down. Relax and be within your space. Look around and take note of any walls, decorations, what are you sitting on, what is around the center space. What is the light source and what is above your position? Take as much time as you like to touch items around you, they're yours after all.

12. At this point, you can interact with your sanctuary in any way you choose. Ask the Divine to help you understand what an object means to you, where is it from, and how can it be utilized today. Try not to do too much that you overwhelm your first visit. You want to remember as much as you can about your space for your first visit. You'll be able to come back as many times as you like to examine everything in your structure.

13. When you're ready to leave, imagine yourself approaching your sanctuary exit. Sitting on a pedestal by the door is a small object. Pick it up and examine it. Make note of what it is, place it in your pocket and then exit closing the door behind you.

14. Visualize yourself passing through the glass doors and heading back down the staircase to your meditative space. Imagine your soul walking into your meditative space and seeing your physical body right where you left it. As your soul steps back inside your physical body, all the visions, sensations, and answers you received merge with your physical mind and are automatically stored into your consciousness.

15. Slowly allow your conscious mind to come back into the room where you're sitting. Feel the chair and floor, feel the room around you, become aware of the subtle sounds and light in the room. When you're ready, open your eyes and take in a deep cleansing breath.

16. This ends the meditation.

Before you go about the remaining activities of the day, record our experience in as much detail as you can in your spiritual journal.

Working With Energy

What Is Energy?

Everything in life has an energy pattern, from the smallest molecule to the largest planet. Science today tells us that, "Energy is an essence of life that forms its existence, fades, restructures its form, and then lives again." Doesn't that describe reincarnation and the process of the spirit/soul?

All energy has certain characteristics to it. It has a sound or frequency, it has a color, and it has movement or a vibration.

Example:

Look at a flame from a candle and examine its entire structure. The brown or black smoke created by the flame, has its own warmth and sound as it travels upward into the air. The yellow flames that flicker on the edges of the fire conduct a warmer heat than the smoke from the flame. Moving closer to the wick you'll see a dark red flame around the top portion of the candle. But you'll also see it sitting on top of a blue flame near the lower part of the wick. Each section of the flame holds its own temperature, one burning hotter than the one above it. Each one has its own sound. Imagine listening to a fire burning in a fireplace, you can here the pops and crackles, and the hisses of heat within the flames. But you can also hear a slight hum or what most people call the roar of the fire.

Modern science also gives us a clue for creating energy. Looking at brain scans of an individual who is relaxing compared to a person who is actively creating art or working on a math problem has shown science the differences in intensity of brain activity. In other words, the different levels of energy created by the brain to work through a task. Albert Einstein has been credited with the statement: "Thought is energy. To create it, just use your imagination." I can't think of a better person to have made this statement. Whither he actually said it or not doesn't diminish the concept.

If we think about energy in this context, it makes it easier to connect to, create, channel, and harness our own divine energy to bring about change in our life. We can create an energy connection to the higher forces through a simple visualization. You can close your eyes and imagine your own immune system fighting off disease or illness in the body. Creative Visualization by Shakti Gawain is one such method of using visualization to enhance any aspect of one's life. Her method and others like it are used to combat illness in cancer centers and other medical facilities in the world today. It's part of a method to treat the "whole" body through the approach of mind/body/spirit healing.

From a metaphysical perspective, we can learn about energy and how it works to enhance our own lives and spiritual path. Have you ever thought about a friend and then had that person call you? We make connections with each other all time with energy and we don't even know it. Why not make a connection to our higher spiritual mind in the same way? You can imagine creating a gateway between your higher conscious mind and the Divine Spirit, and indeed you'll feel it happening.

Exercise: Experiencing Energy

1. Rub the palms of your hands together quickly.

2. Now move your hands apart about shoulder width.

3. Close your eyes and slowly bring your hands together, palms facing each other.

4. Take note of what you feel in the palms of your hands.

5. If you don't feel anything the first time. Shake your hands out, rub them together again and start over. Move a little slower the next time.

6. When you're ready, open your eyes.

What you should have felt was something that feels like a balloon between your palms. This is your own energy, what you can call your energy field that exists around the physical body.

Energy Field Versus The Aura

All living things (people, plants, animals, etc.) are made up of a complex combination of atoms, molecules, and energy cells. As these ingredients coexist, they generate a large magnetic energy field around the physical body. This field can be sensed, felt, and even seen around the physical body.

Like all energy, this field has the same characteristics of sound, color, and vibration. These characteristics are what we know as the "aura." Think of it this way, the energy field is the source. The characteristics of that source are the aura. We sense and feel the energy field, but we can see or hear that field through its aura (or characteristics).

Energy Connection

Metaphysics teaches us that all things are interconnected. We are all connected through energy. Our energy touches the energy of the person next to us and to all living things around us. Consequently, there are varying levels of energy that we walk through each day. Our own energy, the energy of those around us, the energy of nature, the unseen energy from spirits, or the energy of events we have put into motion.

Think about a time when you walked into a room where an argument was going on. You may not know what had transpired, but you can "feel" the energy through the tension or feelings that were being expressed before you got there. You might think of the phrase: "You can cut the tension with a knife" as an example.

"Feeling" Energy

When we talk about "feeling" energy in metaphysics, we're talking about using all your senses. Not just the physical senses, but your energy or spiritual senses. What many know as sixth senses, or psychic senses.

Everyone on this planet is psychic to some degree. Some of us are just more aware of these senses than others. But just like you had to learn as a baby that a stove was hot as you developed your sense of touch, you also have to learn how to recognize and develop your sixth senses as well. There are many types of spiritual senses or psychic abilities, from feeling energy to seeing it, hearing it, smell and tasting it. These psychic abilities are something we all posses at varying degrees.

Using Energy for Good

There are many positive ways to use the energy you create. You can use a quick visualization to protect yourself from outside influences or illness. You can use it for others in a method of holistic healing. You can use it through creative visualization to empower goals, personal endeavors, or spiritual workings.

When you light a candle for your next party, say a little prayer as you light the wick and ask the Divine Spirit to help you create an evening of happy positive energy to benefit the success of your party. Nothing is trivial, and nothing is too big. You have an effect on the energy patterns of the universe as an individual and especially as a group. So give it a try and do some positive creating today.

Energy and the Divine

Because your Divine Self has the energy to create, you have the ability to create your day in the manner in which you desire. That in turn will create your week, your month, your year, and your life. You can create happiness, success, and prosperity in Mind/Body/Spirit. Or you can create negative patterns with your thoughts of hating your job, not liking your boss, or constantly putting down others you know. Gossip is one of the worst forms of creative energy, as it tends to degrade or undermine someone or something else. In creating negative energy, you create negativity around you that will affect your ability to succeed and progress. Not just on a physical level, but through the evolution of your soul as well.

Through meditation we can connect our conscious minds together and create a personal gateway to the Divine Spirit and the energy of Divine Creation. We can use this connection to help us start our day, set the mood for a party, set the tone for a speech or presentation we must give at work, or create the proper energy for spiritual workings.

How To Create Energy

One of the best methods to creating and manipulating energy for changing your life or for spiritual work is through visualization. Knowing the characteristics of the energy you want to create can help you establish that specific type of energy, manipulate it, and send it out for your purpose or intent.

There is no single ultimate listing of energy; it's color and vibration from a metaphysical or spiritual perspective. Many cultures and religions have their own correspondence tables. One of the best methods I've found is the relation of energy and its intent or use to the color and vibration related through the chakra system. We can match up our intended use of energy with the chakra that will help us generate or produce that energy and the color, vibration, and frequency can be defined.

Following is a table linking color, chakra, and energy for workings. This is just a guide; so don't take this as the only way to represent color in your spiritual exercises. Research and practice for yourself to find the best combination for you.

You can use visualization to establish an image within your mind of the color associated with the energy you want to create. If you want to conduct a healing, imagine a clear emerald green light for instance.

Creating Energy

Colors	The Chakra System	The Energy System
White	For Divine Spiritual Work, such as prayer, increasing your spiritual knowledge, meditation, etc.	For purity and/or protection. It can also be used for general magick or as a symbol of the divine forces.
Purple	For Psychic work, such as divination, psychic communication, psychic development, channeling, etc.	For heightened spiritual awareness, self-esteem, and high ideals. Light Purple: For actively working on the balance of each aspect of life (personal, spiritual, professional), attitudes and acceptance of others, and existence with other life. Mid-Dark: For intense spiritual work to evolve ones soul through knowledge and experience.
Dark Green	For matters of the heart, such as love, compassion, patience, heart conditions, etc	For Healing Light Green shades, for the onset or potential emotional or physical injury. Darker Green shades, for an injury that has already occurred and is in the process of healing
Light Green Yellow to Gold	For protection, strength, courage or increasing your "gut feeling" or psychic feelers	Yellow: For clarity, intelligence, wisdom, and success. Gold: For overcoming jealousy, selfishness and negative perceptions.
Orange	For stabilizing emotions, increasing abundance or conducting money spells	For creating confidence, ambition, pride, self-sufficiency.
Red	For grounding energies, increasing physical pleasure, as well as problems with impotence or fertility	For combating fear or anger, self-hatred or negative emotions.

Brown	For Justice, such as helping a law suit, combating a lie or deception	In general, for combating selfishness, deception, confusion or discouragement. Light Brown: For over coming lack of confidence in ones self. Dark Brown: For overcoming selfishness, faultfinding, and a tendency toward deception.
Blue	For working with pride, adoration, or dedication. For masculine emotions, or energies. As a representation of the God. .	For helping to find your way, spiritually searching. Lighter blues generally indicate a beginning of a spiritual quest, a journey that will fill the 'missing' pieces of ones current existence. Darker blues are typically used when one has their spiritual path and is continuing their education.
Pink	For feminine emotions, or energies. As a representation of the Goddess or Feminine Energy.	Different cultures represent love or the heart with different colors; a common American color would be pink for love or red for matters of the heart.
Black	For overcoming hatred, negativity, depression and misery. If used in a ritual for undoing, you can create energies to reverse these emotions.	For undoing a spell that has been cast upon you, for creating confusion or stress (please remember what you put out you will get back. We only conduct spells of undoing when we're working a case with the police. We ask for confusion and stress within the body and mind of the criminal who the police are trying to capture. In this way, we hope the criminal will make a mistake in their actions that will help the police find the evidence, clues and information needed for an arrest and conviction.)
Mid to Dark Green	Financial abundance, security or business matters	For Americans, green can be used for financial abundance. Other cultures may prefer to use a color that represents currency in their country.

Exercise: Energy Visualization

Here is a simple process for creating energy. For this example, we're going to create healing energy.

1. Close your eyes and take in three deep breaths to relax and clear your thoughts.

2. Say a short prayer for what you're intent is in creating this energy.

3. Imagine an emerald green light beginning to glow around your heart chakra. See it moving clockwise at a medium speed.

4. Once you have this imagine in your mind, see the light move through your physical body and gently float into the palms of your hand. As if your heart is creating a ball of green light in your palms.

5. Now you can direct this energy to where you want it to go. Be it a specific part of your own body, another person or living thing, or to a specific situation occurring in your life or around the world.

6. Direct the palms of your hands to what you want healed and imagine the light gently moving; with the same speed you saw it spinning with in your heart chakra to that location you desire it to go to.

7. Continue this visualization for at least 5 to 10 minutes and then release it. Imagine your heart chakra stops feeding the ball of light in your hand. See the ball slowly fading as it sends out it's last bit of energy until it has gradually disappeared.

8. Say to your self; "I let go and let the Divine Spirit take it from here." Or "I let go and let God."

9. Shake out your hands and open your eyes.

The more you work with energy, the more you will be able to feel it and recognize it around you. The easier it becomes to sense events, or other energies that come into your space and the more you will be able to protect yourself, or help others as needed. You'll be able to bring about change through working with your own energies and connecting to the energy of the Divine Spirit as you walk along your spiritual path. And you will be able to work with your Spirit guides and communicate with the spirits around you.

Spirits and Ghosts

There is a difference between spirits and ghosts. Most people lump them both in the same ectoplasm perspective seen in movies, on TV, and depicted in fictional books. But there's a difference between these two types of beings and it's a good idea to understand that difference.

Spirits and Spirit Guides

A Spirit is a being that has crossed over to the spiritual plane of existence. This can be any living thing, not just a person or animal. Plants and trees also have spiritual energy. And it's important not to assume that by "person" we're just talking about Earthly humans. Within Metaphysical practices we also hold the belief that life exists on other planets. Regardless of where a spirit incarnates, the same spiritual laws that we are governed by here on Earth also govern them.

On the ethereal plane, or spiritual plane, a spirit decides how to spend its time between physical incarnations. A spirit can still evolve, learn lessons, pay and redeem karma even in this state of pure energy. But there are still choices to be made in how to accomplish this.

Some spirits decide to provide service to incarnated souls through guidance and support as a Spirit Guide. This is the first group we'll discuss.

During our incarnated physical lives we don't have to go through the emotional, physical, and spiritual lessons alone. Beyond our connection with the Divine Universe, we also maintain connections to our personal Spirit Guides. Whither we know it or not, they are there. They are often the first line of communication when you're talking to that "higher force" outside yourself. And they do try to answer our questions, provide comfort, and aid in our struggles. We may not realize it at times. We may think that voice we heard was our inner mind, or it was just our own overactive imagination that created a picture in our head to give us guidance. But quite often these communications are coming from one of our Spirit Guides.

We have several different types of guides depending on the culture you come from. Each Spirit Guide plays a specific role in our life and assists us in specific ways. Metaphysically speaking, there are five basic categories or types of guides that an individual person may have in their physical life.

1. The Relative Guide

This is usually a person who knew you in this lifetime. Whither you remember them or not doesn't matter. This person is a relative to you in your physical embodiment. Perhaps they are a grandparent, parent, or sibling who has crossed over and helps you through the day-to-day grind and nitty-gritty processes of life. They are the first spirit who greets you at the door when it comes your time to transition from life to death. Your relative guide may change throughout your lifetime as relatives pass and cross over to spirit. You may start out with a Great Aunt, and end up with a Grandparent or Parent as your relative guide.

2. The Spirit Guide

This is usually a person you knew in a past life. This person is on the same spiritual level of knowledge and wisdom that you are on. They help you with your higher purpose and spiritual mission in this embodiment. They help guide you through the karmic issues and spiritual lessons you have chosen to place on your Spiritual Blueprint. They help you learn about the gifts and talents you brought from the past into this life to accomplish the tasks on your blueprint. And they are there for you to communicate with and gain insight from when you need it. Their main purpose is to help you evolve your soul during this incarnation. This guide does not usually change during an individual's lifetime.

3. The Angels

Everyone has a Guardian Angel watching over his or her physical life. This Angel works to protect them and provides a connection to the higher Divine Spirit. It's important to remember that Angels were never incarnated beings. They are the messengers of the Divine and provide both supervision and assistance to many incarnated souls at the same time. This isn't a one-to-one connection, but rather a one (the angel) to many (incarnated soul) relationships.

4. The Master Teacher

If you are destined to be a spiritual leader (it doesn't matter if it's a Catholic Pope, a Metaphysical Minister, or a Spiritual Healer), you will have with you, at the appropriate time, a Master Teacher. This is a spirit who is on a higher spiritual plane of knowledge and wisdom. They help you with the responsibility of "leadership," the dissemination of knowledge and information, the accountability of sharing knowledge, and the higher, more-advanced spiritual evolutionary issues that a leader will need to be aware of. Similar to a Spirit Guide, the Master Teacher is there to provide insight and answers when needed. But they focus on your role as a Spiritual Advisor to others.

5. Animal Spirit Guides

Animal guides come in two forms. Physical messengers and personal spirit guides. Animals in the physical world are here to bring us messages, or show us which direction to take upon our current path. Animal guides in the spiritual world teach us a little more intimate details about our own personality, character traits, and even our spirit and spiritual gifts. They help guide us along our spiritual path, and can even protect us on the spiritual plane as well as the physical.

With the exception of animal spirits, spirits do not appear to us in head-to-toe form. Rather we can only see their form from the torso up. This occurs because the upper chakras are the energy vortices that go with us from lifetime to lifetime. The lower chakras, from the solar plexus down, are renewed with each physical incarnation. It's important to remember this.

Other Spirits

Not all spirits choose to become a spirit guide to an incarnated person. Spirits learn lessons and gain knowledge on the ethereal realm, much as we do here on the physical plane. So a spirit may decide to continue working on its own evolution and enlightenment instead of becoming a guide to an incarnated being.

A spirit might also take some "time off" between the transition of death to spirit and becoming a spirit guide. Taking time to review their life, what they learned and accomplished, and what they have left to work on. This will include a review of karma earned and repaid.

During this time, a spirit may travel the physical world and meet with people they once knew in their last embodiment, or in previous lifetimes. They may visit with psychics and channels and work through those individuals to help teach or share information about the Divine Universe and its workings to a larger group of people instead of just an individual person.

Ghosts

A ghost is basically a deceased being that periodically makes its presence known through a variety of manifestations. Ghosts typically remain in the same general area, not that they are territorial, but rather they remain in locations where they feel most comfortable or the surroundings are familiar. A ghost might attach itself to a person and go where that person goes instead of staying in a specific physical location. They might also attach themselves to an object or collection of objects that they feel connected to and travel with those items wherever they may go.

Ghosts are typically beings that have become tied or bound to the physical plane. They are confused, dazed, or even puzzled because they don't understand that they have crossed over into the spiritual realm. But a ghost can also be tied to the physical through the energy transmitted by mourners who can't or won't stop thinking and talking about the deceased soul. In other words, they become overly concerned about a living person who simply cannot let go of the loved one who passed away.

In these few cases, the ghost is continually reminded of their presence here on the physical plane and they want to remain, either because they didn't really want to leave at the time of their death, or because they are overly concerned about the loved ones they've left behind.

There are a few modern-day examples of these occurrences from the film industry. One of the first was *The Ghost and Mrs. Muir*. In this cinematic account, the Captain didn't want to leave this plane; he didn't want to be deceased, and therefore, he remained in his home. He did have the knowledge that he had transitioned through death, but he tried to use that knowledge to "spook" the new residences out of his home. It's a good example of how a soul who feels they are not ready to go on, will remain in a location that they feel safe and comfortable in. Later in the tale, the Captain falls in love with the physical resident, Mrs. Muir, and chooses to remain on the physical plane to continue his connection with her. At the end of the movie when Mrs. Muir dies, the Captain is there to welcome her into spirit and they both leave the physical plane and enter the white light of the Divine ethereal realm. While the story is presumably fictional, it's a good depiction of how a soul can choose to remain attached to the physical world.

A more recent example is *Ghost* with Patrick Swayze, Whoopie Goldberg, and Demi Moore. This movie was an excellent example of how a soul is taken from their life in a drastic or sudden manner, but remains because of ties or concerns to those they left behind. The feeling of unfinished business may keep them tied to the physical plane, until that business has been resolved. In this account, "Sam" works through outstanding issues to help solve his own murder. Once he is satisfied with the outcome and the concern for his loved ones are eased, his soul is ready to be put to rest and the doorway to the Divine ethereal realm opens to welcome him in.

Another great example of spiritual interaction can be seen in the Robin Williams movie *What Dreams May Come*. This is an excellent depiction of the interaction between souls, karma, choices, and reincarnation as well.

There are a myriad of stories and legends of haunted museum exhibits, houses with ghosts, or more commonly, battlefields where ghosts seem to thrive. These are all good examples of places where souls may have perished tragically and were not ready to transition into spirit. Or they don't realize they have crossed over to the spiritual realm.

Unlike spirits who can be seen from the torso up, when a ghost manifests it is seen from head to toe. Ghosts have not moved on to the ethereal realm and are holding onto their physical existence. As such, they also hold onto the lower chakras, which, as mentioned earlier, are unique and renewed for each physical embodiment. At a battlefield, you might see a Civil War soldier standing in the corner of a room where wounded men were brought for treatment. You might notice his Officer's hat and black knee high boots, for instance. This is a ghost and not a spirit that might also be visiting the same area or refuses to leave for their own reasons.

It's important to note here that just because a soul refuses to leave the physical plane, it doesn't mean they are malevolent beings. Not all ghosts are vicious, mean, or try to harm the living. This is an increased over exaggeration propagated by horror stories and movies. Some souls simply want to be left alone in the location of their death with no intrusive interaction with the living.

Hauntings

The Process of Life and Death

First, we have to talk about crossing over and what that means to the soul. When we begin setting up the spiritual blueprint for an incarnation, we choose certain karmic situations to redeem. We define boundaries that will help us set-up situations for spiritual lessons and growth during the coming lifetime. We even determine how and when we will cross over into spirit again. When a soul completes the journeys set up in their blueprint, they may choose to stay a little while and celebrate or enjoy their accomplishment or they may cross over and continue their journey through other means. But even the adventure of crossing over is aiding in our spiritual knowledge and therefore our evolution.

For instance, if someone dies in this life through drowning, it may be a situation they decided to set-up to have the experience of feeling helpless, or just the experience of the drowning itself. It could also be a way to redeem karma, perhaps the individual who drowned in this life, killed someone or allowed someone to drown in a past life. There are many reasons and ways to view the event, but bottom line, the manner of the crossing into spirit aids in the spiritual advancement and knowledge just like any other physical experience.

When the soul leaves the physical body it is shown the gateway to the spiritual realm. People who have had near death experiences have reported seeing an extremely bright light and a feeling of being drawn to that light. Some report hearing, "It's not your time," and they feel pushed away from that light and then they are suddenly aware of their physical environment.

Even though a soul feels drawn to the light, it's still a choice to walk to it or not. Think of it this way. You are a physical being, you physical body dies, and your soul leaves the physical body. Your soul enters the plane of transition, which is an existence of space and time between the physical world and the spiritual realm. From this point, you are shown the gateway, the bright white light, where you can enter the higher realm of spirit. You can choose to stay on the dark plane of transition, or move toward the light that you feel drawn to. Most move to the light and enter the spiritual realm with no problem. So what about those souls that do not make that choice and move into the Divine light? There are varying reasons why and probably too many to list here. But we can cover a few examples.

Sudden Death

Some souls who are killed, or die before they're ready to go may experience a great sensation of fear or confusion and make the choice not to move toward the light. Some ghosts are taken so quickly, either through murder or accident that they don't realize they have died and don't recognize the white light as a place of warmth, love, and spirit. Some researchers who have studied the process of death have suggested that the soul is plucked from the physical body so quickly or brutally that the consciousness falls into a state of confusion and the person doesn't know what to do. They are for all intensive purposes, stuck between worlds. They then gravitate to the only light that can be seen from this place and that's the physical plane.

The problem with this existence between worlds is that a soul maintains their personality, their desires, likes, and dislikes. They cannot see the spiritual knowledge they hold in their higher spiritual memory because they are blocking the connection to the higher spiritual plane. They also cannot see the Divine knowledge held in their spiritual existence because they refuse to see the Divine light that beckons them to the spiritual plane.

In physical form we can do both of these to some degree through bridging the gaps between each of our conscious minds. We feel the connection to our higher spirit and we can feel the connection to the Divine Consciousness. We as physical beings are open to those energies and have the ability to rationalize the Divine Universe and our place within it. We are able to connect with them, use them, and learn from them. But this isn't the case when a soul has transitioned and let go of the physical part of its being.

It's somewhat understandable then that a Ghost might become bitter and lash out at living souls around them. They can become angry that their own wants and needs are not being met. They long for the physical experience because that's all they know and all they want. They may even realize after a time that they are dead, and they can no longer enjoy the fruits of physical life. But they are still lost or in a state of such despair that they don't know how to continue their journey into the higher spiritual plane.

There are also some souls that might enjoy their situation and become part of the family they are hanging around with. A lot of people share stories of ghosts living in their houses, some scary and vindictive (those seem to be the ones everyone wants to hear about), but others are more kind and friendly. The Universe does maintain a balance, and it's very plausible that there are just as many nice ghosts as there are nasty ones. But the sensationalism of negativity gets the better of the media, which establishes a perception that all ghosts are mean or harmful.

Even those who do lash out might be souls that don't know they have died and they simply hang around the last place they lived. They don't understand what these new people are doing moving into their home and they lash out to protect their property. Think of what you might do if someone simply started moving into your home without your knowledge or permission and you had no way to stop them. You might be angry, too.

Others know they've died, but they weren't ready to go and they are trying to hold on to this existence instead of accepting the transition and moving on. The feeling of ego then takes precedence over their desire to move on to the spiritual realm.

Moving Ghosts To The Light

In all situations, the best thing to do is attempt to help the ghost see the light. To help them understand they have passed on and if they would just look around they'll see the light of the Divine Spirit shining upon a path for them to walk into and transition from the darkness of the physical plane of transition to the Divine spiritual realm.

A single individual can attempt to do this, but it is best to conduct this exercise in a group. Mainly because of the group energy and dynamic can sometimes be more focused and stronger than an individual who might become distracted or afraid. The gathering of people will aid in the combination of energy and help in maintaining the intent of the effort. It is best to have an unmistakable intention to clear the energy of a house, with an underlying intent of helping the soul find its way to the Divine realm. This helps the group stay focused on a positive intent that's achievable and not become frustrated when a ghost doesn't want to see the Divine light. And there can be some pretty stubborn ghosts out there.

There are many ways to clear and cleanse an area. And just as many to helping ghosts see the white light. But here's one possible outline that can be used. Don't be afraid to alter this to your own needs and likes.

Protection And Setting The Intent

As a group or as an individual, the most important step to any process is in the clearing of energy and establishing a level of protection within the area. This can be done with prayer and visualization.

1. Arrange your group in a circle in the area where the ghost has been seen or felt. You don't have to be in the exact room. If a ghost comes to the kitchen, but there's not enough room there, then you can sit in the living room. As long as you're in the same house/apartment you should be fine.

2. Begin by closing your eyes and taking in three deep cleansing breaths.

3. As you inhale through your nose, imagine the white light from the Divine Spirit coming into your body.

4. As you exhale through your mouth, imagine all the stress, anxiety, and worries of you day/week leaving your body. See this stressful energy as a faint gray smoke traveling upward out of the area you are in and dissipating where it can no longer do harm to anyone.

5. Now imagine the white Divine light within your body expanding and connecting to the people on either side of you. Imagine the group setting a circle of Divine energy around itself. See the white light between each person gently moving in a clockwise direction around the circle or gathering.

6. Once this is done, imagine this white energy from each person, connecting at a center point just above the group and in the middle of the circle.

7. As each person focuses on this white light of energy, a cone forms over the group and continues to move in a gentle clockwise direction. Doing these steps help the group set a Cone of Energy (or Cone of Power) that will be used to help the ghost move upward toward the Divine light.

8. Say a special prayer to the Divine Spirit and any personal guides that you may want to come and aid in this process. This can be done out loud, or each person can say their own prayer internally. But at least one member of the group should vocalize a prayer to the Divine as spokesperson for the gathering.

9. The Spokesperson should explicitly state the intent of this gathering. Make it clear that the purpose is to move any negative force or energy from the area (or house) and to set this space in pure divine protective energy.

10. The Spokesperson should then state the underlying intent to help any physical bound souls who are currently in this space, find their way along the path of white light and into the Divine realm where they can once again find peace and love.

The next steps should take into account the following information:

Gathering Information

With the protection set and the intent stated, the gathering can try to contact the ghost and gather as much information from this soul as possible. Who are they, how did they die (if they don't know, ask one of your guides for assistance), and how long they have been deceased. Who were their family members and who do they want to be with now? Perhaps the most important question is why are they here in this space.

Opening the Door to the Divine

Once you have a little information, you can use their story to help them understand the benefits to moving into the white light. If they died in war, you can talk them through understanding that the war is over; their soul can be at peace now. If they were murdered, then let them know the person who killed them has paid the price on the spiritual realm for their death. They were or will be held accountable for their deed. If they committed suicide, then perhaps letting them know that their family is waiting for them in the light, to welcome them and bring them peace and compassion. Treat the conversation just like a therapy session might be conducted for a troubled individual. During the process of communicating with the ghost, you can encourage them to see the Gateway of White Light through the following visual suggestions:

1. Imagine a glass doorway with a pure bright white light shining through into the area you are in.

2. Imagine the cone of energy you established creating a lit pathway to that door.

3. Attempt to guide the ghost toward your circle and looking upward at the path. Talk them through seeing the gateway and help them see the light coming through the door.

4. You can try to call upon any relatives or spirits that might have a significant connection to the ghost. Use whatever information they provided during your initial queries to help them see the path of light, their loving relatives who are beckoning them to look and come toward the light. Encourage the ghost to walk to the gateway and keep emphasizing that they will be okay, they're safe, and they will be welcomed with love and kindness.

5. At some point, the ghost will either walk into the light, or leave the area and run away from the attempt. Don't give up. You can try this again at some other time if the ghost has run away. But when you're ready to close the circle, start with closing the door to the Divine realm.

6. Imagine the door slowly closing and the energy pathway you created slowly falling away and moving back into your circle.

7. Thank all those who came to assist in the effort, both those in your circle and those unseen forces. Then imagine the cone of energy gently dissipating and the connection between participants falling away and fading.

8. Make one final statement to maintain clear positive energy in the area, and continued protection throughout the week/month against any negative force or forces.

9. Make a final declaration, such as: "So it is and the circle is closed."

Each case is different, and will take varying amounts of time to complete. As long as your protection and intent remains, you can help these suffering souls find the peace and happiness they are missing. Most often these souls will find the doorway you have helped to create and they will walk to it. It might take a little coaxing to get them to walk through it, but if you are communicating through love and compassion, you can help them cross over. It is an amazing feeling to help a soul cross into the light. The energy of the house or area is lifted and filled with such love and joy, it's hard to express.

Souls That Cannot Be Helped

There are some ghosts who aren't capable of being helped and these are the ones to be cautious of. You really have to know how to "feel" the energy of a ghost to know if it's just someone caught in the physical realm or if it's a soul with such negative energies and purposes that they are beyond assistance. These are the physically bound entities you should be protecting yourself from when you begin spiritual work, psychic experiences, or channeling of any kind.

If you are in a situation where this might be occurring, you can still clear the space, although it may take some doing and a number of people with a great deal of knowledge and experience. But you can drive away the being and find peace in your own home.

Bottom line, if you feel frightened by a ghost, demand they leave your house immediately. Light a white candle, say a prayer for protection, and ask for assistance from the Divine Spirit and your personal guides. Then stand firm in your own energy. You are just as powerful as they are, maybe more so, because you have the realization that they are dead and that little bit of knowledge can be used in your favor.

Set your demands and use creative visualization to clear and cleanse your house of their energy. Help the souls that are capable of being helped, and clear the ones that can't be assisted or don't want to be helped. Just remember, it's your house. You are the one who is in physical form, and this area or home is a physical structure. You have the right to be here, they don't!

◈✢✧◈✢

Living In Balance

Society in general is taking a good look at how we live our lives in this ever-shrinking world. People look at how they interact with others, how they conduct themselves within business matters, and how much time they spend on making the all mighty dollar and attaining the illusive career. With the implosion of the financial markets around the world in 2007/2008 people were trying to find the right balance of life's daily events and learning what's really important over the materialistic "things" around them.

Like the Great Depression, the Great Recession lead to a return of spiritual values and focus. This had its problems with extremist views, but it also saw a growth in spiritual versus mainstream religious practices. People became more concerned with living in a spiritual mindset, instead of adhering to old rules or static thinking. The world, especially the West, saw an increased growth in metaphysical and pagan beliefs, which continues today.

In many ways, this explosion of spiritual awareness can be linked to the changing impact of the Cosmic Cycles discussed earlier. And if those cycles are accurate, it's a pattern that will continue for a long time to come.

The Balance of Life and Spirit

Many people are searching for something "bigger" or "more meaningful" within their lives. Many look outside, some inside, and some to higher forces. As a person becomes more aware of their desires to find a spiritual nature that fits within their concepts of divinity and faith, a lot of things begin to change in their lives. And sometimes, maybe more than not, people suddenly become very critical of themselves.

Perhaps it's because the common idea of what a "spiritual person is" can often be far beyond our capabilities to attain. We look in a mirror and condemn ourselves for something we did that was "non-spiritual." We may say I've "fallen from grace" and then beat ourselves up about it later. But we try the next day to aspire to the illusive image that we've created in our mind once again.

It's great to have lofty goals, as long as you can attain some of them once in a while. But one thing to remember is that our soul is only 50% of who we really are. We are also 50% human, and as such we have human desires, needs, and emotions. Those human traits are not always conducive to spiritual thinking or spiritual ways of living. But we don't have to beat ourselves up about it.

There is some validity in the old adage: "Too much of a good thing can still be bad for you." It's very true. Living to much in the spiritual mind and not being grounded isn't any better than those who live in the physical world and never give their spiritual natures a second thought, or a first one, for that matter. It's an adage that tries to define the parameters between living in the extremes and living in balance.

What we are here to learn above all, is balance. Through that lesson, you can learn acceptance, and how to let go of the past to move on into your greater future. Letting go doesn't mean loving those who hurt you, rather it means forgiving them within yourself and then letting go of the emotions to move on. As I have said earlier in this book, "You cannot change the past. All you can do is change the way you allow the past to affect your present and influence your future."

Many people think being a spiritual person means you don't cuss, you don't lie, you don't have bad thoughts, and you don't drink, do drugs, or talk about sex. To some, you don't even have fantasies, or get angry, or even say a bad word about anyone. Now if that's living as a spiritual person, then no one on this planet can call them selves spiritual. Being someone who is always pushed around emotionally because you believe that's what living as a spiritual person means, isn't living in balance. Perhaps your lesson would be to learn how to stand up for yourself, believing you have rights and your own emotions have validity.

If someone makes you mad, then accept the emotion for what it is. It is a human emotional response to a personal situation. Now isn't that what you're here to learn about? Aren't we here to experience human interactions and emotions on all levels in order to learn? How are you going to do that, if you don't "feel" any emotions?

Balance is learning to control the extremes.

Living in balance means keeping that anger in perspective. You don't take it out on someone else and you don't try to kill or physically harm the person you are mad at. You just accept the emotion for what it is. If you lash out at the person who made you mad, then you will have to accept the consequences of the energy you created by doing so. You are allowing them to control you and your response to their actions. Don't give them the satisfaction of taking your power away from you. Better to accept, let go, and allow the divine laws of karma to provide justice. If you act upon desires to avenge your emotions, you will be no better off than the person who hurt you.

I'd like to note, we're not talking about physical crimes here. We're talking about personal emotional issues. If you believe someone has harmed you physically, then we urge you to contact the authorities in your area.

Spiritual Living

Spirituality is one of the most personal and intimate things about the human being. It cannot be forced within your being. If you don't believe in something, no matter how hard others try; they will not control your mind and inner beliefs. People must decide for themselves what they believe in life and in their spiritual practices. The key to defining who you are and who you want to be is looking within and discovering the respect for self, others, and all things seen and unseen around you.

With respect, you can accept the views of others, even if they don't agree with yours. You can attain tolerance for alternative perspectives even if they fly in the face of what you believe. By learning respect for yourself, you lose the need for the "I'm right, you're not" ego. What others believe cannot force you to change what you believe unless you allow it to. If you respect your choice, than nothing anyone else can say or do will be able to threaten your beliefs and your inner connection with the Divine Spirit.

In living by this principle of respect you can attain inner peace. You can easily take the steps necessary to go within and rise above the fray of the physical world and view events through spiritual eyes. You will be able to ascertain the spiritual reasons, lessons or karmic experiences that have created situations in your life. And you will be better able to handle them in peaceful loving ways that benefit your path to spiritual enlightenment.

Resources

Alper, Dr. Frank. *Universal Law.* Arizona Metaphysical Society, 1986

Ibid. *Exploring Atlantis.* Vol. 1, Publisher: None Stated, 1982

Ibid. *Exploring Atlantis.* Vol. 2, Publisher: None Stated, 1982
ASIN: B0012ZOSMS

Andrews, Shirley. *Lemuria & Atlantis: Studying the Past to Survive the Future.* Llewellyn Publications, January 2004

Artress, Dr. Lauren. *Walking A Sacred Path.* Riverland Books, 1995

Barrett, David. *Sects, Cutls & Alternative Religions.* Cassell Imprint, 1996

Belhayes, Iris. *Spirit Guides.* ACS Publications, 1986

Berlitz, Charles & Crest, Fawcett. *Atlantis: The Eighth Continent,* Ballintine Books, 1984

Bletzer, June G. Ph.D. *Encyclopedic Psychic Dictionary.* Dunning Publishing, 1986

Brady, Joan. *God On A Harley.* Pockett Books, 1995

Cameron, Julia. *The Artist's Way.* Perigee Books, 1992

Cayce, Edgar Evans. *Edgar Cayce on Atlantis.* Warner Books, 1968

Cranston, Sylvia and Williams, Carey. *Reincarnation.* Julian Press, 1984

Eden, Donna. *Energy Medicine.* Penguin Group, 1998, 2008

Ibid. *Energy Medicine For Women,* 2008

Foundation For Inner Peace. *A Course In Miracles.* Foundation For Inner Peace, 1975

Gawain, Shakti. *Living In The Light.* New World Library, 1986

Ibid. *The Path Through Transformation.* Nataraj Publishing, 1993

Ibid. *Return To The Garden.* New World Library, 1989

Ibid. *Creative Visualization.* Bantam Books, 1982

Goodwin, David. *Cabalistic Encyclopedia.* Llewellyn Publishing, 1997

Knight, J. Z. *A State Of Mind, My Story.* Warner Communications, 1987

Langley, Noel. *Edgar Cayce On Reincarnation.* Warner Publishing, 1967

Laurie, Sanders and Tucker, Melvin. *Centering A Guide To Inner Growth.* Destiny Books, 1983

Lusson, D.D., Rev. Michelle. *Creative Wellness.* The Printed Voice, 1992

Ibid. *Spiritual Psychology I.* Course Work, 1994

MacLaine, Shirley. *Going Within.* Bantam, 1989

Marciniak, Barbara. *Bringers Of The Dawn.* Bear & Co., 1992

McLaughlin, Corinne & Davidson, Gordon. *Spiritual Politics.* McLaughlin & Davidson, 1994

Moody, Jr., Raymond MD. *Life After Life.* Bantam Books, 1975

Purcel, Jach. *Lazarus: The Sacred Journey.* Concept Synergy Publishing, 1987

Ibid. *Lazarus: Interviews Book 1.* Concept Synergy Publishing, 1988

Puryear, Herbert, Ph.D. *The Edgar Cayce Primer.* Bantam, 1982

Roman, Sonya . *Personal Power Through Awareness.* HJ Karmer, Inc. 1986

Ibid. *Living With Joy.* HJ Karmer, Inc. 1986

Ibid. *Spiritual Growth.* HJ Karmer, Inc. 1989

Roman, Sonya and Parker, Duane. *Opening To Channel.* HJ Karmer, Inc. 1987

Stone, Joshua David, Ph.D. *The Complete Ascension Manual.* Vol. 1, Light Technology Publishing, 1994

Ibid. *Soul Psychology — Keys To Ascension.* Vol. 2, Light Technology Publishing, 1994

Teilhard de Chardin, Pierre. *Activation of Energy: Enlightening Reflections on Spiritual Energy.* Harvest Books, 2002

Notes

Notes